Mastering the Art of Learning

POWER GUIDE TO A GREAT EDUCATION

■ Secrets of the "A" Maker ■

Incredible Grades for Average Students

Darrin King

Mastering the Art of Learning
Published by Noble House Publishing, Inc.
1972 NE 3rd St. #21 Bend, OR 97701

http://www.NobleHousePublishing.com

Library of Congress Catalog Card Number: 00-191829
ISBN: 0-9646807-1-8

Printed in Canada

CONTENTS

AN INTRODUCTION TO THE GAME

Allow me to introduce myself. My name is Darrin King, and I am one of America's most successful students. The primary purpose of this course is to coach you in the strategies and learning techniques that will lead you to success in college and beyond.

In the pages that follow, you will learn the rules of the game that determine your grades in school. The rules are very simple - anybody can understand them. I'll show you the little known, and even less used secrets of success in school. You'll learn how, when, and where to apply the most powerful techniques to make the grade. *However, the decision to use what you learn is completely up to you!*

You, and only you, are responsible for every grade you make. If you expect to simply read this book and presto! get straight A's without any work on your part, then you, my friend, may as well stop wasting your time reading. You need to learn the hard reality of life: there ain't no such thing as a free lunch. When you decide you're ready to work, believe me I'll be the first one to show you the way. If, on the other hand, you are already committed to working to improve your grades and your future, then congratulations, you're already on your way! Read on.

There's only one way to learn anything. Do you know what that way is? Think about it for a minute. Remember when you learned how to drive a car? It took plenty of trial and error to find out how the car handled, how it responded to your motions. The only way you learned was by experiencing the impact of your actions, correct? Experience is the only way to learn.

Imagine that when you learned to drive, you moved to a different country and also had to learn a whole new set of traffic rules. Would you want to learn by trial and error? That could quickly become very expensive! "Oops, officer, I didn't know I was supposed to drive on the wrong side of the road." You get the idea. How would you learn in this situation? Take a ride with someone else? Maybe take a driving class? In short, you wouldn't waste your time learning the rules all by yourself through trial and error. You'd seek the experience of others who already know the rules.

College has its own unique set of rules. You don't learn them at freshman orientation. Nobody passes out a brochure that says, "Guess what, folks? The college game is different from anything you've ever experienced before, so we've decided to list all the rules for success in college!" Kind of hard to play the game without anyone telling you what the rules are, isn't it? That's exactly the reason I'm here. I can hear you now - you want to know what makes me so special, why I think I know the rules. Good for you! That means you understand it's important to learn only from those who have produced the results you desire. Fair enough. I'll tell you about me for a minute or two.

I went to college at the second-best endowed school in the world, with the largest number of National Merit Scholars in the country at that time: the University of Texas at Austin. Most of my courses were part of an honors curriculum that selected the best students out of 35,000 undergraduates and pitted them against one another in competition for grades. I earned an A in every class I took - more than forty courses in all. I produced these results in fine arts classes, social sciences, foreign languages, literature, mathematics and other natural sciences; in seminars, laboratories, lecture classes, self-paced courses, and independent study/thesis classes. I have succeeded in virtually every type of college class. Just so you know I didn't spend 25 hours a day studying, I earned these grades while I was in varsity athletics (crew) and while I had a part time job as a teaching assistant. I even had time left over to have a girlfriend! I graduated as one of the Dean's Distinguished Graduates, first in my class (4.0 GPA) of many thousands, and as Phi Beta Kappa's Outstanding Achiever. Guess what else? I graduated college 2 years and 8 months after the day I first set foot in a college classroom.

After missing a perfect score on the GRE (graduate school's equivalent of the SAT) by just a couple of questions, I applied to 7 of the top 15 graduate schools in my field: economics. All the schools not only admitted me, but also offered me a free ride, to the tune of about $750,000 altogether. We're not talking about run of the mill schools, either. Those seven schools were MIT, Stanford, Princeton, Berkeley, Caltech, Northwestern, and UC San Diego. I was also awarded the coveted National Science Foundation Fellowship for Graduate Study - an all expenses paid three year trip to any graduate school in the country. If you want to know the secrets to producing the results you desire in school, I'm your man! I won't load you down with a lot of abstruse theory on getting good grades - that would be boring and useless. I'm going to tell you the nuts and bolts, the hard facts about what works and what doesn't. I'm going to show you how to make the grade in any situation you face.

You're probably saying to yourself, "Yeah, this King guy may have been able to ace college, but he was born a good student. He just made good grades because he was smarter than everyone else." Thanks for the generous compliment, but.....you're wrong! Wrong! Wrong! You become a good student through decision, training, and work. If intelligence determines grades, then why did Albert Einstein flunk out of grade school? Because he was stupid? I doubt it. He didn't play the game by the teacher's rules. That's the only reason for not succeeding in school. Maybe school bores you, or perhaps you don't know or like the rules, or you could just be plain lazy, but the only reason you have ever achieved less than fantastic grades is because you didn't play the game very well. Period.

Learning and performance ability simply are not innate characteristics. The foundation of good performance in school is a set of skills and strategies that must be learned, practiced, and used - the techniques you will learn in this book. Sure, some people may have certain genetic advantages over others, but no one, and I mean no one, uses anything close to his or her potential. I'm sure you've heard that we use only 2% or 5% or 10% of our mind's potential. Well, that's an inaccurate and irresponsible statement. No scientist has been able to quantify for certain the absolute potential of the human mind, so it's ridiculous to say we use a specific percentage. How can you calculate the percentage used if you don't know the total mental ability? The basic message has merit, though. Since none of us uses his full potential, any of us can do better than someone with a larger potential by using more of what we have available. Simply put, anything anyone else can do with his mind, you can do with yours. Let's talk about how amazing our minds really are.

The human mind's ability to learn and remember is virtually limitless. Every experience you've had, everything you've ever learned, is stored inside your mind. Experiments performed by Dr. Wilder Penfield confirm this wondrous property of your mind. Dr. Penfield applied electric current directly to the brains of his patients and discovered that while the current lasted, the patients were able vividly to relive experiences from the distant past that had long since faded from conscious memory! Subjects recalled childhood birthday parties as if they were happening all over again. Do you realize what this means to us? Every single one of us has a fantastically powerful mind that can potentially recall everything we have ever experienced! Your mind can store and recall literally billions of pieces of information. This doesn't apply just to mental prodigies and phenomena - we all have basically the same wiring upstairs. Apparently what limits us in unlocking our abilities is the image we hold of ourselves and what is possible for us. Consider this example of a classful of young students.

Psychology researchers had an entire class of students take an IQ test. Instead of giving the students their actual scores, however, the researchers deliberately falsified the results. Students who had scored average on the tests were told that they had performed far above average. The teachers, like the students, were led to believe the fake scores were accurate. The end result after several weeks of school and a second IQ test? Guess. Yes indeed, the new scores of the "smart" students actually increased to what the students had been misled to believe were their IQs!! They believed they were smarter than average, so they performed smarter than average. If you simply allow yourself to believe in your abilities, to see yourself as a good student, you will become what you see in your mind's eye. Your self image determines your ability.

You see, the ability to make excellent grades is already within you. You merely need to give yourself permission to achieve by believing in yourself. The training you receive in this book, if you practice and use it, will unlock your potential. Your mind has the incredible ability to do exactly what you tell it to do. If you tell it that you're stupid or that you can't do math, it listens. It literally will act stupid if your self image dictates that it should do so. On the flip side, if you tell it that you're smart, and give it good reason to believe it (use the new skills in this book) then guess what? Your image of yourself changes and with it, your performance in school.

Given average mental ability, the student who makes better grades has a better attitude, more determination, better study skills, more efficient use of time, and a better working knowledge of how the grading system operates than his classmates. This book will show you the way to remedy any shortcomings you have. Bad attitude and the will power and direction of a leaf in the breeze? Check out Chapter 1 on goals to light your fire. Poor memory? Chapter 7 teaches the best time-tested memory techniques known to man. Pitiful study skills? Don't know how to perform under pressure? Chapter 9 will be a godsend. These are just a few of the topics dealt with in this tome. You'll gain more new strategies for success than you can imagine, including: how to take a professor for a test drive, the best way to prepare for the hardest classes you'll ever take, how to start off your semester like a wildfire, the way you should really listen to a lecture, how to memorize a lecture without taking notes, methods of talking to your professor for maximum effect, how to write the perfect college paper, techniques to help you ace every type of test you will encounter, how to read to understand much more in less time, ways to eliminate test anxiety forever, how to graduate from college in 3 years, the keys to getting spectacular letters of recommendation and much, much more. Every chapter will introduce to you to a few of the 140 Rules of the Game. When you finish this book and use everything you learn, you will be an absolutely unstoppable A-Maker! Now, let's get started...

FINDING YOUR DIRECTION

1 What do you want to do with your life? Ouch, that's some way to start a chapter! We can go no further together until you answer this question. Can you be motivated to succeed in school if you have no idea what good school is doing for you? Of course not. We're just going to have a seat until you figure out why you're in college or why you want to go to college.

Do you have a deep love of learning coursing through your veins that drives an insatiable appetite for knowledge? Or maybe you aspire to be a capitalist robber baron and make piles of cash? Do you desire to better the condition of your fellow man as a social worker or third world missionary? Just looking for your Mrs. or Mr. degree, perhaps, and want to make the wait as easy academically as possible? For the purposes of this course, which answer you give is not important - only that you have a *definite* answer. I'm coaching you on the tactics to make mega grades, but before you will decide to use the tactics, you must have direction - some type of motivation to do well in school. Let's find out what motivates you. Answer for yourself all the questions I'm about to ask. If you're serious about improving your grades, *do not skip this or any other exercise in this book.*

1. Where do you see yourself in 10 years? Don't worry about me, I'll wait until you have an answer you like. Take all the time you need. I'm serious - this exercise is very important. OK, if you said, "Still in college" that's the wrong answer! Try again! I'm talking to the future you now: what do you do for a living? Is it your dream job? Do you love it so much that you'd do it for free? If not, go back and try again. Find something that really, really means the world to you. Choose a life other than what you truly

desire and you simply won't be excited enough about your future to make any real effort in school or any other endeavor. You owe it to yourself to give this subject some very serious thought right now. If you're just reading straight through all this without thinking, put the book down and walk away. I can't teach you a thing until you're willing to go to a little trouble and THINK! Turn to the Exercises section in the back of your course and complete the first exercise immediately.

**Rule #1 Find a future that excites you
and motivates you to take action now!**

Proffefial conic Book Artist

2.

College is important to me because I can make connections w/other people and perfect my skills ~ + learn *how* to learn; and create a hunger for knowledge.

■ Do You Need to be in College?

I will assume you now know where you want to be in 10 years. Tell me about your job. Does college contribute anything essential to your preparation for your perfect occupation? If you want to be a doctor, dentist, attorney, engineer, teacher, etc. the answer is an obvious yes. But say you'd like to fly a hot air balloon or a crop duster, or maybe you'd like to be a lumberjack or any of a huge number of other things - four years of college may not be the wisest choice for your future. You will of course always continue to learn as long as you live, but college is only one place you can learn. If college is necessary for you, think about your future and write down a statement to yourself that explains why college is important.

2 Exercise Two awaits you in the back of the course. Do it now. The rest of this book is geared toward college students, but anyone who wants to learn more efficiently can benefit greatly from reading and practicing the techniques here. If you've discovered you don't belong in college, start taking the steps necessary to create the life you want. If you'd like to continue reading, we're glad to have you along for the ride.

Now you're starting to see the Big Picture. You know what career you want and you know what value college has for you. It's time to pick a major. What major will provide you with the best possible preparation for your career? College is a means to an end, so treat it as such. The journey can be tons of fun, but it's primarily meant to prepare you for your future. If you're not already certain what major is best (and even if you are certain), talk to a few people from the real world who are already living your dream. Get their input on your education. If you show your respect for their experience, believe me they'll want to help you. You'll probably learn much more than you bargained for. Do not overlook or underestimate the importance of this step. Immediately write down the names of some people you know who do what you want to do, or the names of some people who could introduce you to someone you should meet. Take action now. Complete Exercise Three.

intern/ job Shadow

**Rule #2 Build a group of advisors
from the field you want to pursue.**

Let's hope you now know your major. Did you know there are a few habitual questions that different types of graduates ask after college? Natural science students are inclined to ask, "Why does it work?" Engineering students ask, "How does it work?" Liberal arts students ask, "Would you like fries with that?" Ha ha ha! I have a liberal arts degree myself. I won't ask though, because fries are bad for you. Onward...

■ A Blueprint for your Education

Our next step is to create a master plan for your college education. Optimize the time you spend in school. Take control of your education and don't let anyone else exercise any power over you. You're investing four years of your time, thousands of dollars, and countless hours of hard work, so YOU determine your plan and stick to it.

**Rule #3 Seize complete control
over your education immediately.**

Look ahead to the day of your graduation. Remember last chapter when I was so long-winded about my accomplishments in school? I want you to step into your future again and write a one paragraph announcement of what you achieved in college. Make the announcement describe you as you want to be, as you know you can be if you work for it. What degree did you earn? What honors? To which organizations did you belong? What kind of grades did you make? Where are you headed now? You get the idea. Impress yourself with how well you did! Take just a couple of very effective minutes and do this exercise now. Turn to Exercise Four.

Now complete Exercise Five. Assume you don't have any direction, that you only make haphazard, random efforts in school, and that you don't read this book and practice the techniques I teach you. By some chance in 6 years you manage to graduate. Write your announcement, and keep it short. Just humor me and amuse yourself for a minute. Get a very clear idea of where you're headed if you don't work for it. Won't you, your friends, and family be oh, so proud?! OK, which announcement do you prefer? Stupid question. You control your outcome here. If you'd rather make the first case your reality, read on and I'll show you how.

You know why college is important to your future, you know what your major is, and you know the details of the outcome you want to produce. Now all that's left to do is to make the blueprint for your education. Get your college catalog out - the one that describes your graduation requirements. Learn your requirements as well as your own name. You have to take responsibility for getting the classes you need for graduation when you need them. Don't rely on your counselor to think for you. Use Exercise Six to make a blueprint that describes what classes you will take every semester until graduation. Some of the classes are dead end requirements, others are essential prerequisites. Attach special priority to any class that is required before you may enroll in other classes you need. Decide that you will take the classes when you need them, and don't let anything stop you. Next you'll learn how to create a goal for every semester, every class, every test, every paper. With the aid of your blueprint, you'll understand how all these goals fit together as the building blocks of the future you want.

■ *How to Set a Goal*

What is a goal? What you shoot the basketball through or the hockey puck into? Well, yes, actually it is. A goal is a specific, concrete, measurable objective. If your goal is to learn "faster" or to make "better" grades, then you don't have a goal. You have a indefinite wishy-washy lukewarm desire. If you want to achieve something, you have to tell yourself exactly what it is you want, and exactly when you want it. Make a single, concise sentence for any objective you have, and write it down on paper. "Make better grades" becomes "Earn an A in Professor Zimic's Literature of the Western World class this fall." "Learn faster" is now "Double my comprehension by actively rereading Chapter 2 on Reading Skills, then applying the techniques at least twice daily for the next three weeks." Do you get the idea?

**Rule #4 A goal is a specific, concrete,
measurable objective that you find exciting.**

Set high, but attainable standards for yourself. "Make a C in Psych" is just not a very exciting goal, is it? Only big goals such as "Earn a 4.0 GPA this semester and make the Dean's List" can give you the motivation to take the necessary action and follow through. A definite, exciting goal will help you release your own power. There is one catch, though. Once you gather your facts, make an evaluation, and commit to a concrete, measurable, written goal, you have to take action - immediately. Unfortunately, no goal achieves itself. That's where you come in...

**Rule #5 Goals are nice,
but they don't achieve themselves.**

Action plans are the key to achieving your goals. Let's build some of these academic power tools, shall we? I call this technique reverse visualization. Picture in your mind the ultimate result you wish to produce. Since your goal is very specific and measurable, this task should be a piece of cake. Now, take one step backward in your visualization. What happened immediately before you achieved your goal? Be very observant. Say your goal was to make an A in Professor Zimic's Literature class this fall. Well, immediately before you made the grade, you took a final exam and aced it! Yeah! Good job. Write the step of acing the test underneath your goal. OK, keep going backward. You turned in a terrific term paper during the final class. Write that down too. Find everything that stands between you and the attainment of your goal. Each of these items is an opportunity to take one step closer to your goal, so make the most of it.

**Rule #6 Use reverse visualization to discover
what you must do to achieve your goals.**

Making an A on that term paper may seem like a difficult task to you, so break it down into more manageable, smaller tasks and give each one a deadline. The whole project is much less daunting when it's reduced to: Pick a topic by October 31; locate six good sources by November 7; read and take notes from all sources by November 21; construct a thesis and outline by November 28; fill in details on first draft by November 30; edit and polish paper December 2, and turn it in the next day. Don't you think you could easily handle all of these steps if you made a plan at the beginning of the semester? Everybody knows what happens if you don't plan. "Oh, $#%@, my Lit term paper is due in 2 days! Well, I only have to write 8 pages a day, no problem." You run yourself ragged for 2 days and then turn in a huge pile of manure with hopes that the prof will think it smells sweet enough to pass you. Then you think, "I will never, ever do that again!" Yeah, right.

One reason students put off papers and studying until the last moment is that the thought of the entire project is extremely intimidating. The solution is so simple! Take your blueprint for success each semester, visualize in reverse to outline all necessary steps, and break everything you need to do into manageable, friendly little tasks that you can accomplish easily.

(Baby steps)

Rule #7 Large projects are much more easily achieved when broken up into manageable pieces.

If you expect to achieve your goals, you have to set up a plan of action that allows you to take a step toward success, no matter how small, every single day. Your goals are only idle dreams until you make a plan and take action. If you spend too long planning and mapping out every step, though, all you're doing is engaging in a sophisticated form of procrastination. Take action!

Rule #8 Make action plans that allow you to take a step toward your goals every day.

■ Tips for Achieving your Goals

You can greatly increase your goal achieving effectiveness if you learn to master and use three very important concepts: visualization, self questions, and persistence. We'll discuss all three in turn.

A goal can only be achieved when it is pictured clearly in the mind. Doctors and scientists have written countless books on the topic of visualizing your goals for better performance in sports, business, relationships, and just about every other aspect of life people would like to improve. Perhaps the best of these is *Psycho-Cybernetics* by Maxwell Maltz, M.D. I can't hope to cover all the points here, so it will have to suffice for me to say that if you want to achieve, you absolutely must provide your mind with a very clear, detailed vision of your goal as if you have already attained it. See, hear, feel, smell, and live your reality as you wish it to be. Keep the vision of your goal in your mind at all times. After all, "As a man thinketh in his heart, so is he." Your thoughts become your reality.

**Rule #9 Use your mind frequently to create
a detailed vision of your goal attained.**

The speed of your success is determined by how frequently you visualize your goal. I always perform my visualization exercises twice a day, morning and night, and also occasionally during the day. Visualization provides your mind with a goal toward which it can continue to strive, even when you are not thinking about it consciously. Seeing yourself attaining your goals also increases your motivation and self confidence. If you want to achieve, visualize your goals.

Another very powerful technique is to use the Jesuits' test of conscience. Several times during the day, ask yourself this question:"Are my current actions taking me closer to my goal?" Think carefully and answer yourself truthfully. If the answer is "No" then change what you're doing immediately! Of course, I don't mean for you to have zero leisure time. Some time to relax and have fun does take you closer to your goal - it preserves your sanity. If, however, you're just piddling around to avoid work by shooting the breeze, surfing the web or watching television, you won't be able to avoid the answer to the question. A good way to remind yourself of what you should be doing is to keep your most important goals on a notecard in your wallet or pocket. When you ask yourself the question above and discover you're wasting time, pull out the notecard, read the goals, and think about what achieving each of them means to you. If you're not willing to work for them, scrap the goals and start over. You need to find something that motivates you to take massive action.

Rule #10 Evaluate your actions periodically to make sure you're consistently working toward your goals.

The final and most important key to achieving your goal is simple, but not easy. Calvin Coolidge describes it best:

Nothing in the world can take the place of persistence. Talent will not. Nothing is more common than unsuccessful men with talent. Genius will not. Unrewarded genius is almost a proverb. Education will not. The world is full of educated derelicts. Persistence, determination and hard work make the difference.

As you head toward your goal, you're certain to run into obstacles that will require you to make a few course adjustments. Whenever you encounter adversity, the sole factor that will determine whether or not you succeed will be your persistence. You must ask for what you want, show tremendous determination, and keep asking. You may have to try different approaches, but keep gunning for what you want. How you handle your struggles will define your character. As Conrad Hilton once said,

Good timber doesn't grow with ease.
The stronger the wind, the stronger the trees.

Rule #11 Your persistence above all else will determine whether you achieve your goals.

■ *Your Potential*

Who's responsible for your outcome in life? Hopefully you said, "I am!" Every time you flip on the television or read the newspaper, you see some new group of "victims" with their hands out, lamenting their poor state in life and demanding that someone else take responsibility for their lives. It's so incredibly sad to see an able bodied, able minded adult refusing to take charge of his life and use his assets as reasons to achieve rather than his liabilities as excuses to fail.

**Rule #12 You, and only you, are responsible
for every result in your life.**

Within you is the ability to achieve any goal you desire. You just have to want it enough to do whatever it takes. Starting today, forget every limiting experience of your past. Plant your feet firmly where you are and decide to move forward. Your future will be determined not by your past, but by what you do today to develop yourself.

**Rule #13 Your future will be determined not by
your past, but by the actions you are taking right now.**

Life demands only one thing of you (no, not taxes). Life requires that no matter who you are, where and when you live, or what you do in life, you must live with the consequences of your decisions and actions. If you want to succeed in school, the actions you need to take are all in this book. Are you willing to decide to pay the price of effort and hard work? Answer me. If "Yes!" is your answer, let's get to it...

**Rule #14 You must live with the consequences of
every decision you make and every action you take.**

There were a total of fourteen rules introduced in this chapter. If you're serious about making straight A's in school, take a couple of minutes and complete this short exercise. Go back through the chapter and rank the fourteen rules in order of importance for you. Record your ranking here:

1. _____

   _____

2. _____

   _____

3. _____

   _____

4. _____

   _____

5. _____

   _____

6. _____

   _____

7. _____

   _____

8. _____

   _____

9. _____

   _____

10. _____

_____

11. _____

_____

12. _____

_____

13. _____

_____

14. _____

_____

READING EFFECTIVELY

2 Reading is the first skill discussed in this book for three important reasons. First, good reading skills are the foundation of all learning. If you can't read well, you are severely limited in school and life. Second, most students simply don't know how to read effectively. They've never been taught. Finally, you have a whole book in front of you on which to practice these reading skills. The more you learn and use the techniques in this chapter, the better you'll understand and recall the rest of the information in this book.

Before you begin reading anything at all, know your mission. Ask, "Why am I reading this? What do I hope to gain?" Are you reading for maximum retention for a test? Are you searching for some specific fact for a research project? Or are you seeking a general understanding of a broad subject? Different missions require different reading methods. You wouldn't want to read every word of a long book if all you need from it is one piece of information.

**Rule #15 Know your mission
before you begin reading.**

The methods in this chapter are best used when you need to understand and retain information. The reading system I recommend is a five step process represented by the acronym PUCR-UP. Other reading systems abound, including the best known SQ3R system developed 50 years ago. My system places a different emphasis on the aspects of reading that are most important for college students. PUCR-UP stands for Preview, Understand, Concentrate, Recite, Use, and Presto! you understand and remember.

Rule #16 PUCR-UP for effective reading!

■ *Preview*

This step is fairly obvious. What do you do when you look at a book for the first time? You preview the book by checking out the title, jacket summary and author info, the table of contents, preface, forward and introduction. Read it all and you have what amounts to a preview of the book and the author's purpose. Everybody already does this, right? The single most important difference between good learners and bad ones is the organization of material prior to learning. Previewing the book, especially the table of contents, helps you organize the information in advance.

Rule #17 Organize information before you try to learn it.

The essential step that almost all students miss is, as one famous radio personality often states, "The rest of the story." The title, preface, foreword, summary and author information all attempt to cast the book and its creator in the most positive light possible. Of course, you would too if you were trying to sell a book, correct? You can often locate your book and author in other reference sources to discover the full background of the author and to find out what critics thought of the book. Find the *Book Review Digest* and *Contemporary Authors* in the reference section of your school's library and look up any book you're using in class or for a research paper. Make sure you have a full perspective, both positive and negative, of the work and author before you start reading. Keep this perspective in mind as you read and evaluate the information presented.

**Rule #18 Get to know the book and author
before you start reading.**

■ *Understand*

This step carries the preview even further. The task here is to understand exactly where the author is coming from. What questions is the author attempting to answer? What underlying assumptions has the author made in order to pose these questions? Are these assumptions valid? Are the author's sources of information reliable? Are the author's conclusions based on opinion, fact, reason, or experience? What is the author's bias? Everyone has some sort of bias. If you ask and answer all of these questions, you will understand the author's perspective and be much more likely to grasp and remember what you read.

**Rule #19 Understand the author's goals,
assumptions, methods and biases.**

■ *Concentrate*

Now it's time to start reading. Look over the whole chapter to get an idea of structure. Are there plenty of subheadings? Summary at the end? Questions at the beginning or the end? Read all of these things first to discover what the author considers to be the main points of the chapter. For every chapter, make a written note of these main points/questions. When you go back to the text, use your reading time to find out how the author arrived at his conclusions. Concentrate on finding the main points and linking them together.

Most importantly, relax with the highlighting! Most students seem to think the book is on fire and only highlighter ink can put it out. Unfortunately most college students read to find out what to highlight rather than read to understand. If you just dive into a book without previewing or understanding what the author is trying to do, you end up marking everything as important, and all you have achieved is a small financial contribution to the company that makes the pens you just used up. Concentrate instead on the author's main points - the answers to his questions. Highlight only these main points and the arguments he uses to arrive at his conclusions. That's all you really need to remember.

**Rule #20 Discover the author's main points
and highlight only the information that contributes
directly to those main points.**

■ *Recite*

The purpose of recitation is to get you personally and actively involved in what you read. Have you ever had the experience of reading an entire page of a book while your mind wandered, only to discover that you couldn't recall a single word? Of course you have! Recitation keeps your concentration on the text in front of you and increases your comprehension and recall by leaps and bounds. Would you like to learn how?

After every paragraph you read, pause for a few moments and state in your own words the meaning and purpose of the paragraph. At the end of each section, restate the purpose of the whole section as concisely as possible. Simple? Yes, but incredibly powerful! You literally force yourself to pay attention actively, constantly questioning the author's purpose and seeking important points. Let's say you can read a chapter in a book in thirty minutes. If you spend a full hour reading and reciting as you go, you will learn and recall many, many times the amount of information you would if you read the same chapter twice. Recitation works so well because it requires concentration, active reading, repetition, and provides feedback on how well you are learning. Recite what you read, and your reading comprehension and recall will soar!

Rule #21 Pause after each paragraph, section and chapter to recite in your own words the author's main ideas.

■ Use What You Learn

The final step in this power reading system is using what you learn as quickly and frequently as possible. Take out a clean sheet of paper and attempt to recreate as accurately as possible the author's flow of thoughts through his work. Create from your memory the outline he must have used. If you recited as you read, this task will not be very difficult. Now, take a look at the most important points that the author made. How can you relate those main thoughts to other books you've read? How about to the lectures in class? Do the ideas relate to things you've learned in other classes? The more things you can relate to what you learned, the better you'll recall the information over the long haul.

**Rule #22 Recreate from memory an outline
of the main ideas in the work.**

Now take those main points and use them. If you're in a math class, use the axioms you just learned to prove a theorem. If you're in a literature or philosophy class, apply the main themes to answering essay-type questions your professor has discussed in lecture. If you're reading a history book about the development of Japanese society, compare and contrast the author's principles to those of a totally different society with which you're familiar. The possibilities for using what you learn are literally endless. They're limited only by your creativity and commitment to learn. Once you use what you have learned, you own it permanently. Presto!

**Rule #23 Apply what you have learned to a problem
immediately after you finish reading.**

■ Fiction

The reading system described above is most useful for nonfiction, which for most students represents about 90% of college reading. I'd never dream of neglecting the other 10% though, especially since fiction can be among the most interesting and valuable reading you can do. The main thing to remember when reading a work of fiction is that it's all about people. How many novels have you read that didn't revolve around the lives of people or other creatures put in a human-type perspective? I rest my case. Since the lives of people are the most important aspect of fiction, what do you think you should pay most attention to when reading? Hmm. How 'bout the characters? Make a character analysis sheet for every person you encounter in the work. Describe their looks, personality, profession, role in the book, etc. Treat the character likes he's a real person and get to know him. Trace the life of each character: at the end of each chapter make a few notes on each character's page to remind yourself what happened. Attempt to stay one step ahead of the author by predicting developments. When you're finished with the book, note what you learned. Think of the themes the author was trying to emphasize with the lives of the characters he created. Every author is trying to tell you something about life, so figure out his message. The professor wants to know how well you ferret out and understand these themes, so expect essay questions and papers that give you an opportunity to show what you know.

**Rule #24 Fiction is all about the lives of characters.
Understand the characters to discover what the
author is trying to tell you about life.**

■ *Vocabulary*

How quickly you read and how well you understand what you read are influenced tremendously by the size of your vocabulary. Guess what else? A large American business did a study to determine the size of its employees' vocabularies and discovered that the larger your vocabulary, the higher your rank in the corporation and the larger your salary. Isn't that interesting? If money motivates you, think of every new word you learn as a few extra dollars you earn! Here's a powerful technique to help you increase the size of your vocabulary rapidly. I'm sure you've heard the basics before...here goes.

Keep a vocabulary notebook with you anytime you read. When you encounter a word you don't know, write it down in your notebook. When your dictionary is handy, record the definition, pronunciation, part of speech, and origin. Memorize the word using one of the fantastic memory techniques in Chapter 7, and then find a way to use the new word several times the next day, even if it makes you feel silly. Amaze your friends with your new knowledge! Insult strangers without their even knowing it! At the end of every week, review all the new words for the week. Once a month, look over your entire list. Practice this program everyday and soon you'll read with greater speed and understanding, your test scores will increase, your writing will improve, you'll polish and advance your conversational skills, and you will actually think better. How? Well, is thinking any more than asking and answering questions? You had to think to answer that, see? Improve your vocabulary and you'll be able to ask better questions and discover more enlightening answers.

Rule #25 Keep a vocabulary notebook to improve your reading and writing ability, grades, and conversational skills.

OK, now you know how to learn and remember what you read. I expect you to apply these techniques for the remainder of this book. Remember what the last step to more effective reading is? Use what you learn.

There were a total of eleven rules introduced in this chapter. Record your ranking here:

1. _____
_____

2. _____
_____

3. _____
_____

4. _____
_____

5. _____
_____

6. _____
_____

7. _____
_____

8. _____
_____

9. _____

_____

10. _____

_____

11. _____

_____

PLANNING YOUR SEMESTER

3 College is very serious business. Let's just talk in terms of cold hard cash for a few minutes (here comes the economist in me). You'll spend four years in college, during which time you could have made approximately $80,000 to $100,000 had you chosen to work. College will cost you anywhere from $20,000 to $100,000 in tuition and books alone. That's a total cash investment of between $100,000 and $200,000! When you pay, say, $200 for clothes or $50 for a nice dinner, do you just take whatever is available, or do you shop around and make sure you get what you pay for? What about if you were shopping for a $20,000 car? Would you visit several dealerships and haggle for the best deal? If you don't, you're either not playing with a full deck or money simply isn't a worry for you. Don't you think since you're spending between $100,000 and $200,000 on college, you should put a thousand times the aggressive effort into making sure you get exactly what you want? So few students do! They simply move along calmly like a herd of cattle to slaughter. Think of your university as a business and yourself as a paying customer. You absolutely must demand to get your money's worth from every class and every professor. This chapter will show you how to get maximum value and effect for the time and money you invest in your education. You have to plan your education and control what you get every step of the way. It's totally up to you to make your college experience worthwhile.

Rule #26 Think of your university as a business and yourself as a paying customer. Get what you pay for!

■ *Pick Your Classes*

Typically there's not much room to maneuver here since degree requirements are very specific. From Chapter 1 you already have a good idea of what type of classes you need to get your degree. Three important points still remain though. First, many a student has fallen victim to an extra year of school simply by missing an important prerequisite early in college. Know your degree requirements and fight for the classes you need when you need them. Remember, you're paying for your education, so demand the classes you need. Don't let some pompous administrator tell you, "Sorry, the class is full. Try again next semester." With enough determination, tenacity and plain old hard-headedness you can get whatever you want. More on this later after we've talked about picking your professors in advance.

Rule #27 Know your degree requirements completely. Fight for the classes you need when you need them.

The second point is to choose classes, especially electives, based on what you like rather than what has a reputation for being an easy class. This book may be about how to get straight A's, but an A in a worthless underwater basket weaving class is a senseless waste of your time and money. Good grades are almost guaranteed in a class you have a real passion for, even if the class has a reputation for being the hardest on campus. Go with what you love, use the techniques in this book, and the grade will follow "as the night must follow the day."

Rule #28 Good grades come easy in classes you love.

Finally, check out your school's catalog to find out which classes offer credit by examination or which classes have a self-paced option. I used these devices to graduate from college in less than three years. CLEP tests, Advanced Placement tests and each individual college's tests for credit are fantastic ways to avoid spending a great deal of time on classes that don't interest you very much or those that are just a repeat of high school work. One summer I took a community college self-paced class in Texas history to satisfy a state graduation requirement, and I finished the class in one week with three hours of work per day. That was the quickest A I ever made!

Rule #29 Take advantage of your university's credit by examination program and self- paced classes to graduate more quickly.

■ Pick your Professor

Almost no students do this intelligently! It's amazing!! The best analogy I can think of for picking a professor is buying a used car. Why? Because you never know if they're any good unless you take them for a test drive. Never, ever assume a professor is a good teacher just because he happens to be employed by your university. Some are complete jalopies! Lots are foreign jalopies that can't even communicate lucidly in English. I'm sorry, but if I'm paying $20,000 a year in tuition and spending fifty hours in a class during the course of the semester, I'm going to make damn sure my professor can at least speak clearly in the language in which the course is supposed to be taught. Many other professors couldn't care less about teaching - they view it as a necessary evil because they're only interested in their research. If you want to pay for teaching assistants with master's or bachelor's degrees to teach you, you may as well go back to high school. Luckily, good professors abound. You just have to work to find them.

Rule #30 Professors are like used cars: the only way to know if they're any good is to test drive them.

Let's take a prospective professor for a test drive. The first step is to pay the professor a visit during office hours. Tell him you are considering taking his class next semester and you'd appreciate a few minutes of his time to ask some questions. Be courteous and respectful throughout this entire process. You basically want to discover if you like the professor's style of communication, assess whether or not grading will be fair, and see if the teacher is enthusiastic about his subject. Tell him you take your education very seriously, and since you will spend about 150 hours of your time working on his course, you want to make certain you spend it wisely by selecting the right professor and class. A whole battery of questions follows. Add more questions of your own if you like.

- How does your class topic fit into the larger picture of economics, or literature, or history, etc. ? (insert your discipline here, of course!)

- What are the most important themes of your subject?

- What major points do you stress in your class?

- Do you teach the class yourself, or do TAs carry the teaching load?

- Are you accessible outside the classroom? How many office hours do you have each week?

- On what basis do you determine grades? Tests, papers, class participation, etc.?

- What are your qualifications - both in your subject and teaching in general?

- Do you have any references, any past students with whom I could speak?

- If more than one professor teaches the same course: Why should I pick your class? Why is it a better investment of my time than the alternative?

- May I attend a lecture of yours this semester?

- May I have a copy of your course syllabus and reading list?

Be a very good listener! Maintain eye contact at all times, nod to show him you're listening, and don't interrupt at all. You're making your first impression on the professor you may have next semester, and believe me it will be an unusually good first impression. Professors are not accustomed to seeing students who express a sincere interest in learning.

The tests, homework assignments, and paper guidelines are invaluable indicators of what you can expect next semester. Do anything necessary (honestly, of course) to get your hands on as much information regarding graded material as possible. Some professors will give you the information readily, but sometimes you have to go to former students.

If the class you're taking is extremely important as a prerequisite, pick the professor that will provide you with the best coverage of the subject regardless of how hard he grades. You'll be grateful when later classes are a breeze instead of a struggle. On the other hand, if the subject is a dead end graduation requirement that doesn't interest you, try to find a way to test out of it. If that fails, take the easiest grader and save your valuable study time for classes that matter more to you and your future.

Rule #31 If the class is important for your future, choose the professor who will provide you with the best education. If the class is an unimportant, uninteresting requirement, choose the easiest professor.

Now that you've selected the best professors and classes, register as early as possible to make sure you get the courses you want. If you don't get in on your first attempt, persist. Go see the professor in person again and express your interest in taking his class. If you did your work recommended above, the professor will remember you very well, and lucky for you persistent and interested students are attractive to teachers. He'll be flattered that you chose his class, so he'll help you get in. Another good idea is to register for one more class than you intend to take and then drop the class you like the least after two weeks.

Rule #32 Register for one more class than you intend to take, then drop the class you like the least.

Finally, if you get the opportunity to take multiple classes from the professor of a class you did well in and enjoyed, by all means do so. A good grade is almost guaranteed, and you'll also be cultivating a very valuable source of a recommendation letter. The only drawback is that you could have exposed your mind to a new professor with a different outlook, but the benefits outweigh this one drawback in my opinion.

Rule #33 Take multiple classes from your favorite professors. Good grades and fantastic letters of recommendation will result.

That's the best way to get ready for an important game? You wouldn't just show up and pray you performed well, would you? Hopefully you'd prepare yourself in advance. Get to know the game so you know what to expect, maybe practice a little, right? Every college class you take is a game from day one, but most students show up with no preparation whatsoever. Next you'll learn how to ready yourself to play the game well.

■ *Prepare in Advance*

If you've followed my instructions so far, you already have the syllabus and reading list for the class before you even register for it. Once you decide on the class, ask the professor if he plans to make any changes to the textbook selection, then make a trip down to the bookstore and buy your books early. If it's currently fall, you have the winter break to get a little head start. If it's spring, the whole summer awaits you. Familiarize yourself in advance by previewing all the books for the class and reading and reciting the first few chapters of the main text. It's fine to give yourself a rest over the holidays, but don't go completely brain dead. Simply take an hour or two a day to get ready for the next semester and you'll be way ahead of the other students.

**Rule #34 Buy your books early and read the
first few chapters in each before class begins.**

Is there an extremely difficult class you have to take? If there's some class you fear because everyone fails it, I have a plan to make you the one who aces it. Audit the exact class you plan to take the semester before you register for it. Act as if you're really taking the class. Sit in on every lecture, take notes, take every test, and write the papers. Treat it like a real class, and when you enroll in it for real you will know exactly what it takes to make an A. It's so much easier to learn a difficult subject the second time around.

**Rule #35 Audit an extremely difficult class
one semester in advance.**

■ Make a Master Calendar

After the first two days of the semester, you should have a good idea of when your papers will be due and when tests will be given. Get any calendar big enough to write on and record the dates of anything that has an impact on your grade. Use a different color pen for each class. If some dates aren't certain, then highlight the time periods you believe are most likely. Now record the dates of everything you can think of that will place a demand on your time. Parties, athletic events of all sorts, you know what I mean. I will never advocate that you plan every minute of every day. That would drive me nuts, personally. You should always make time for fun and refuse to let school intrude. I just want you to get a very good idea of where any potential conflicts exist. College can be a real juggling act, so make sure you have a big ol' calendar to guide you.

**Rule #36 Make a master calendar so you can spot
and plan for all potentially dangerous time conflicts.**

Using your calendar, construct an action plan for each class on a separate sheet of paper. Remember how we broke the task of writing a term paper into several easy tasks back in Chapter 1? Use the same procedure to give yourself a rough schedule of deadlines for every major assignment you have in each class - tests, scheduled homework assignments, and papers. If you have three papers due in different classes all in the same week, you'd better know about it from the first week of class so you can plan accordingly.

**Rule #37 Use your master calendar to create
an action plan for each class.**

Do you know how the Grand Canyon became such an incredibly awesome sight? Every single drop of water that travels down the Colorado River carves out just a minuscule amount of rock from all that surrounds it. No single drop's effect is very great, but the cumulative, relentlessly consistent effect of all those drops over time has sliced an enormous chasm in the face of this planet. Take every class one small, manageable step at a time and you can carve a similarly impressive result in school. Look at your action plans at the beginning of every week. Make any adjustments necessary, and then rank the tasks you need to complete that week in order of importance. Tackle the most important things first, not the easiest ones.

Rule #38 Consult your action plans each week and take action to complete the most important tasks first.

Be careful not to overplan. Both doing easy tasks first and overplanning are just sophisticated ways to procrastinate. All you're doing is putting off real action. The types of assignments you're likely to delay are the ones that will become bigger and bigger in the back of your mind every day that you fail to act. Eventually the difficult tasks will weigh so heavily on you that they'll interfere with your ability to have fun outside of school, and that is completely unacceptable. The only way to solve the problem is to determine the most important action you can take to carry you toward your goals, and then do it - immediately!

■ *Take Off Like a Shot!*

Give it all you've got until the first test in each class. Overlearn everything until you know it like your own name. Until that first test comes, you never know for absolute certain what to expect, so put out that extra effort for a few weeks while your motivation is still high. Maybe the class will turn out to be easier than you thought and you can relax a little. Perhaps the first test will be so hard that it will blow everyone away - everyone except you that is, if you prepared for the class in advance and gave full effort for a few weeks. No matter what the situation, you're better off if you work hard for a little while. Believe it or not, it won't kill you.

**Rule #39 Full exertion at the beginning of
each semester pays off big.**

After you've exerted yourself for a reasonable amount of time, don't hesitate to cut your losses short. If, despite all your planning, you find yourself in a real loser class, drop it before deadline! Give the class and professor the benefit of the doubt for a couple of weeks or until the first test, but trust your judgment and bail on a class you don't think will be worthwhile. Remember, you're in charge of your education. You call the shots.

Rule #40 Cut your losses short - drop that loser class.

Well, now you are taking your education seriously, selecting your professors carefully, preparing in advance for the class, planning your semester, and committing yourself to maximum effort for the first couple of weeks of class. Let's find out how you can spend the time in class most effectively.

There were a total of fifteen rules introduced in this chapter. Record your ranking here:

1. _____

_____

2. _____

_____

3. _____

_____

4. _____

_____

5. _____

_____

6. _____

_____

7. _____

_____

8. _____

_____

9. _____

_____

10. _____

_____

11. _____

_____

12. _____

_____

13. _____

_____

14. _____

_____

15. _____

_____

SCHOOL DAZE

4 Most college students sit through class (when they attend, that is) in a mental fog. Some students spend their time checking out other students, some sleep off the previous night's party, and other poor misguided wannabe good students try to record in their notes every word the prof says. Very few students pause to think about how they could turn their school daze into time effectively spent. This chapter will show you what to do before, during and after your classes to make the grade.

■ *Prepare Before Class*

What does your professor do for you before just about every lecture to help you prepare? He gives you a reading assignment on the topic, right? Always, always, always complete the reading assignment before you go to the lecture! Almost without exception, the reading assignments will provide you with background knowledge that is essential to getting the most out of the lecture. The professor invariably thinks that his comments on the topic are more important than those of the author he has you read in advance (unless he is the author!), but his lecture takes for granted that you already have a foundation that will enable you to see why he's so much more clever.

**Rule #41 Completing and understanding
the background reading assignment before the lecture
is essential to your success in school.**

If you've read the selection and thought about it, the lecture will become much more interesting, you will pay more attention, and the second treatment of the topic will reinforce what you have already learned. If you haven't prepared, you may waste a whole hour being completely lost. In addition, you won't know if what the professor is saying is important and needs to be noted, or if it's just a repeat of the reading. You're investing thousands of dollars and hour after hour of your time, so make sure you at least come to class prepared to learn.

■ Go to Class!

Every grade you make in college is a measure of how good a salesman you are. You have to sell the professor on the idea that you deserve an A.

Rule #42 If you want an A, you have to sell the professor on the idea that you deserve it.

Of course, your best opportunity to convince him you deserve an A is on tests and papers. If, however, you're on the grade borderline, it helps a great deal if you have sold the professor on the idea that you're a serious, sincerely interested student who makes a real effort. The first step you took forward building this image was taking your professor for a test drive. Your next chance to contribute to your image is to attend class at every opportunity. Does a serious student ever show up late or leave early? Do you want your professor to think you're a serious student? Then the course of action should be obvious. Always be there when class starts, and never leave before it ends. Important announcements are usually reserved for the beginning or the end of class, so be there, OK?

Rule #43 Be in class on time, and stay until the end of every single lecture.

Where should you sit in class? "Oh, great, now he's gonna tell us we have to sit in the front row and be the little teacher's pet. Next we'll probably have to raise our hands to answer questions and yell, 'Ooh, ooh, ooh! Pick me!' to get the professor's attention." You're partially correct - I am going to tell you to sit as near as possible to the front of the classroom.

However, it's not the professor's paying attention to you that I'm worried about, it's your paying attention to the professor. If you sit in the back of the class, it's a virtual certainty that there will be several attractive people between you and the professor. So, you're a college student with raging hormones, there's some extremely hot girl or guy two rows up and to the left, a boring old professor talking about something you're not terribly interested in at the front of the class, and you're supposed to pay attention to the prof? Please! Don't lie, you know you're not listening to your professor. The nearer you sit to the front, the fewer distractions you must endure.

Rule #44 Minimize distractions by sitting in the front of the classroom.

What's the best way to listen to the lecture? Actively, the same way you should now be reading. Don't depend on the teacher to make things interesting. Some are so dry and lifeless it makes you wonder who figured out how to animate a mummy. Take an active role and seek out something that you can make interesting. Anticipate where your professor is headed. Read between the lines of what he's saying and look for his true meaning. In order to do these things, you have to be a very good listener. First rule of good listening: keep your mouth shut until called on to speak - don't interrupt anyone. Second rule of good listening: give total attention to your professor. Always look him in the eye when he talks. Nod your head when you agree. Get a puzzled expression on your face if he loses you. In short, show him you're alive and listening! Most students will be off in a daze or trying to record everything said. If you show you're paying attention and that what he says matters to you, you will build an even more favorable image. Sales, my friend. It's all sales!

Rule #45 Show your professor that you're alive by listening attentively and actively.

How should you take notes? Sparingly. You should spend at least 75% of your time actively listening, thinking, and searching for the professor's main points - the things that will be on the test. For most students, note taking replaces thinking during the lecture. You're not a stenographer taking a dictation - don't write down every word spoken. Your professor will probably only have five or ten major points in his lecture. Find these main thoughts and construct an outline. They're not hard to find. Your professor will pause, emphasize them, write them down. He'll do something to hint at the importance of the point. When test time comes, other students will have to wade through volume after volume of notes to find the important stuff to study. All you'll have to do is pull out your notes and tell yourself how clever you are.

Rule #46 Spend 75% of your time in lecture listening to your professor to find his main points. Spend the other 25% writing those points down.

How much should you participate in class? The answer depends in large part on the professor's way of conducting class. I had one pompous ass for a professor that would state at the beginning of the lecture that there would be NO questions and NO interruptions because we should be grateful to have the opportunity to hear him speak. He regarded any student's remark or question as a terrible waste of time. At the other end of the spectrum are professors who consider themselves to be facilitators of student discussion. They believe we learn more by testing our thoughts against those of our fellow students. Obviously, you wouldn't participate at all in the first scenario, but you would be expected to carry your own weight in class every day in the second situation. I have a few good rules to govern your participation that apply to all the courses and professors that fall in between. The first rule is never make a nuisance of yourself. Everybody hates the pest that sees the need to comment on everything discussed. You know who you are - learn to control your tongue. Second, the meek may or may not inherit the earth, but they certainly won't make the grade. Don't be afraid to speak up in class. You need to earn the respect of the professor to get the grade. You won't do so by refusing to open your mouth. So, the first rule is don't speak too much, and the second is don't speak too little. Find a reasonable middle ground and make what you have to say count. Above all, be courteous to your professor and your fellow students.

Rule #47 Make your presence in class felt, but never be a nuisance.

What should you say in class? My favorite thing to do, and it's a very effective way of selling the professor on the idea that you deserve an A, is to ask intelligent questions that illustrate you have done the reading assignment. If you truly understand your reading, you'll be able to understand the areas in which the author and your professor disagree. When the professor says something that contrasts with the opinions of the author, raise your hand and ask him to explain why his views and the views of the author diverge on this point. Figure out what the implications of this difference are for the topic you're studying and discuss it with the professor. If you can't find any disagreements, remember something important that you read that the professor hasn't discussed, but that relates to the lecture. Ask what importance the professor attaches to the point. Make it clear that you've done your homework and that you're interested in the topic.

Rule #48 Ask questions that show the professor you're a serious, interested student.

■ After Class

As soon as possible after class, review your class notes. If you took notes for maximum effectiveness, you only recorded the main points. Sit down in a place where you won't be disturbed and think carefully about the lecture and its main points. How do they relate to one another? How does this lecture fit in with the last few lectures? What possible questions could the professor ask about this information on a test? Record any questions you come up with after your notes. Now try to fill in the major details from the lecture under your main points. Create the outline that the professor probably used to construct his lecture. The procedure of immediately reviewing and organizing your class notes will help you remember the lecture better than anything else you could possibly do. The effectiveness of this exercise is greatly enhanced if you can do it within one hour of the lecture. An additional benefit of this practice is that you can immediately find any areas of the lecture that you don't understand. Ask your teacher about them during office hours or right before the next lecture.

Rule #49 Within one hour after the lecture, review, organize and fill in your notes.

■ A Few Final Notes

Your dorm or apartment is a den of distractions. In between classes you may usually go back home, but your time will probably be spent much more effectively if you leave your room before your first class and don't return until you've reviewed your notes for your final class. Use the time between classes to review or prepare for your next lecture in some quiet place where you won't be disturbed like the library or any empty classroom. If you spend your time wisely, you may finish all your work for the day between classes and get the night off to have some guilt-free fun.

Rule #50 Don't return to your dorm room or apartment between classes. Use the time to review your previous lecture or to prepare for your next one.

Reading before class and reviewing afterward are actions you have to commit to and perform consistently if you want to learn as painlessly as possible. Never fall behind in a class. The effort required to catch up is much greater than the effort required to stay ahead. If you miss a lecture, don't prepare in advance, or don't review you're just making it harder to make an A. Why not make it as easy as possible instead?

Rule #51 Always keep up in every class.

There were a total of eleven rules introduced in this chapter. Record your ranking here:

1. _____
_____

2. _____
_____

3. _____
_____

4. _____
_____

5. _____
_____

6. _____
_____

7. _____
_____

8. _____
_____

9. _____
_____

10. _____
_____

11. _____
_____

A FORMULA FOR
FANTASTIC PAPERS

5 Whether you like it or not, writing papers is a very big part of any college education. I know of only three actions that will help you improve your writing: read more, write more, and learn the techniques in this chapter. Good writing skills are so important in upper level classes and in the working world that you should try to take as many writing classes as you can early in your college education. Those classes will help you with the first two actions: reading and writing more. This chapter will distill the wisdom and techniques used to create literally hundreds of A papers. Read it, learn it, and use it.

**Rule #52 Take as many writing classes as you can.
They're good for you.**

■ *Thesis*

The first, and arguably the most important, step of every writing assignment is defining your thesis. The thesis is the basic premise of your paper - your purpose for writing. A good thesis has four properties. First, it must be interesting to you. How motivated will you be to research and write about a topic that bores you? You can find something of interest within any topic at all if you try hard enough. If you regard all the topics available as dreadfully dull, find a way to link one of them to a subject that does interest you. I built many A papers in literature, government and history classes using generalizations of economic theories and principles of mathematics. The papers were often highly unusual, but creative and attention getting. One of the best papers I've ever written applied a principle of wave propagation from physics to Ovid's *Metamorphoses*. The professor of the honors literature course was so impressed he asked me to read it aloud to the class. Look hard enough and you'll find a novel way to link the subject to something you really enjoy and understand. Of course, it helps if your professor thinks it's interesting as well.

**Rule #53 Find an unusual way to link your paper topic
to something that interests you.**

The second property of a good thesis is that it is narrow and specific enough to be answerable in the space available to you. Obviously you can't prove a thesis regarding the reasons for the collapse of the Soviet Union in a two page paper. Keep the thesis reasonably simple, then stun your professor with your ability to prove it in a new and unexpected way.

Third, a good thesis is researchable. Make certain you have access to the information sources you will need to prove your point. A couple of interesting ways of coming up with sources when the outlook is grim will be discussed in the research section of this chapter.

Finally, a thesis must be open to debate. College papers usually require you to state a position on a debatable issue and then use your wits and all available resources to show that your position is most reasonable. In a history class, you may have to prove which factors were crucial in determining the course of a few events. In a literature class you could demonstrate which themes were most important to an author using several of his works. In a psychology class you may have to establish which paradigm explaining certain mental functions is more useful for evaluating the results of an empirical study. One way or another, you have to put yourself and your views on the line and then marshal your resources to show a preponderance of evidence in your favor.

There you have it. Your thesis must be interesting to you and your audience, it must be narrow and specific enough to answer thoroughly, it must be researchable, and it must be open to debate. If your thesis has all of these properties, your problem is well defined and the battle is already half won.

Rule #54 The ideal thesis is interesting, specific, researchable and debatable.

■ Research

The key to good research is locating and using unusual sources of information that other students simply don't make the effort to find. Where do you usually begin when you research a paper? Students typically start with the library catalog and encyclopedia. Not a bad start, if it truly is a start and not a finish. You have to look beyond the average research sources if you hope to achieve an above average grade. Your first step beyond is to ask your research librarians for help on your topic - helping you is their job. These individuals can offer incredible insight into any research problem you're tackling. They know more about where to find information than anyone else. After you pursue the leads the librarian supplies, check out these additional four sources of information very few students use.

First, rifle through the footnotes and references in any good book you're using for research. If the author quotes a source, it's a good bet you'll find useful information there as well. Make your way all the way back to original sources to really get the feel for a subject.

Second, if your topic is likely to have been handled in any way by the popular media (magazines, for example), look into the *Reader's Guide to Periodical Literature*. Also look for journal-style academic treatments of your topic in the database for the appropriate discipline. Several of these databases are available in just about any college library. Ask the librarian to show you how to work them.

Third, try out the web search engines available to anyone with an Internet account. www.dogpile.com or www.yahoo.com are good places to begin any search. Try many different keyword searches for your topic to make sure you get as wide a variety of relevant websites as possible. Also make full use of Gopher, Telnet and FTP to access additional sources for your paper. Ask one of the campus computer consultants how to operate these utilities if you need help. There's no end to the interesting information you'll come across on the Internet.

Finally, the least exploited resource: people. Find a few knowledgeable people outside your own university. Perhaps you can contact the author of a book or a journal article about your topic. Maybe you can find experts at a museum or in the faculty of another college. Consider the authors (the living ones, that is!) of all your sources as potential people to interview. Depending on your topic, you may be able to find a very interesting variety of individuals to contribute to your paper. If you start your paper early enough and formulate interesting questions for these individuals to answer (questions they have not already answered in their works), you can count on the participation of at least a few of them. A telephone call or simple email could result in just the right embellishment to your paper - that special something that will make your paper stand out in the mind of your professor. Be creative!

Rule #55 Go beyond the average sources if you expect more than an average grade.
Make use of research librarians, footnotes, academic databases, the Internet, and interesting knowledgeable people.

■ Stew Time

After I've constructed my thesis and done all of my research, I just let all of the information stew around in my mind for a few days without any active effort to think about the paper at all. Give this a try, assuming you begin your paper early enough to use this powerful technique. After you've finished your research, write your thesis in big bold letters at the top of a piece of paper. Read all of your research notes through one time. Now briefly jot down the few main points you plan to use to establish your thesis on the rest of the page. Place everything relevant to your paper in a folder and set it aside for a couple of days. It's best to do this just before you go to sleep at night.

Do you know what's going on in your mind once you've done this? Your subconscious actively works on any problem you present to it, most frequently when you're not thinking about the problem consciously. When you write down your thesis, you're essentially making a statement of the problem you want solved. When you read your research notes, you're giving your mind the raw material from which to create a solution. Haven't you ever had the experience of suddenly, out of the blue, remembering a piece of information you were trying hard to recall earlier in the day?

Or perhaps having a solution to a troubling problem pop into your head once you gave up trying to find it? That's exactly what you're giving your mind a chance to do for you when you take a break from your paper for a couple of days. Be certain to have a pen and paper ready to record the sudden flashes of inspiration you'll get. Write down everything, now matter how silly it seems at the time. If you wake up with an idea at night, take the trouble to turn on a light and write it down - you'll never remember in the morning.

**Rule #56 Enlist the aid of your subconscious
to write a better paper.**

I know some of these techniques may seem a bit strange, but believe me, they work. I have a huge stack of A papers to prove it!

■ Outline and Write your First Draft

A very effective way of taking advantage of the ideas your mind has come up with in the last few days is to create a free form outline. Write your thesis in the middle of a large blank page of paper. Without consulting your notes, branch out in all directions with pieces of information you can use to establish your thesis. Every piece of information gets a little node all to itself somewhere on the page. After you've exhausted your imagination and memory, pull out your research notes and go through them from start to finish, adding nodes to your free form outline.

Next, link the nodes together with one another in the ways that make the most sense to you. Link together all of the related points that you will use to construct one part of your paper. The main ideas become branches radiating from the thesis in the center, and individual details are the twigs extending from the branches. Your piece of paper may be a tremendous mess, but your thoughts will be much clearer after this exercise.

Finally, transfer the primary idea of each of the main branches to a new piece of paper. Don't worry about the details until a little later. Link these main ideas together as best you can. We're building transitions to make the flow of your paper as smooth as possible. What ways can you think of to link the branches together into a coherent whole that proves your thesis? Work on this until you have a satisfactory way of giving an order to the branches and linking them all together. Write down a sentence describing the link between the points. Congratulations, your outline is finished and you're almost done with your first draft!

**Rule #57 Create a free form outline
to link all of your ideas.**

Writing your first draft is simply a matter a getting down on paper, in order, the ideas that you just developed. Don't be too worried about an intro at this point - just get something with your thesis in it down on paper. Now move on to each of your branches in sequence. What are the twig details that contribute to this branch? Go back to your free form outline and find the relevant twigs. Start of with a statement of your main point for this branch, then weave the twigs into a coherent body paragraph. Finish the paragraph with the transition sentence you developed in the second linking exercise. Move on to the next branch and repeat until you've covered all the main branches. Throughout this entire stage, write as quickly as you can. Pull out all the stops and don't even think about proper grammar. We'll deal with all of that later. Now just get a rough idea of how you would like to close the paper. Don't even think about writing, "In summary..." if you want that A! We'll talk more about good closers later. Time to kick back and relax - you're done with your first draft.

**Rule #58 Write at maximum speed -
worry about grammar later.**

■ Critique and Revise

Get some distance from your first draft. Let it rest for a couple of days so you can be more objective in evaluating it. Pick up the draft and act as if you've never seen it before now. It doesn't belong to you, you just have to critique and correct it. Before you correct grammar, concentrate on ideas. During your first reading you should check to see if the assertions made in each paragraph contribute directly to the thesis of the paper. If not, ax 'em. If the assertion is relevant to the thesis, demand definite concrete proof that the assertion is accurate. What cold hard facts are there to support the claim? Are there any examples, illustrations, metaphors, analogies or contrasts that prove the point? If not, the point is weak and must be strengthened if you want an A. Are the transitions between different parts of the paper smooth and logical, or does the paper seem to jump randomly from one topic to another? Your goals should be organization, clarity, and simplicity. You must provide a trail of hard proof leading inevitably from your thesis to your conclusion. Do yourself and your professor a favor: leave out the BS. If there's anything your professor has learned in his years of teaching, it's how to detect the stench of college students' BS from a mile away. Be very hard on your paper. Your professor will be looking for all these flaws too. If you let any of these things slip, your professor won't.

**Rule #59 Critique your paper harshly.
Require organization, clarity, and concrete proof.**

For your second reading, concentrate on the grammar of the parts of the paper that survived the first reading. Never let a single awkward word or phrase escape your editing. The topic of correct grammar and usage is far too large to deal with here. All I can say is learn the rules. No excuses! You may not like the language or the rules, but your grade definitely will be influenced by how well you express yourself according to the rules of English grammar and usage. I'll deal with a few major points of writing style in a later section.

**Rule #60 Learn English grammar and usage.
There are no excuses for ignorance.**

■ *Everything is Sales!*

Remember that point? You have to sell your professor on the idea that you deserve an A. Your paper has to compete against every other paper in the class, and unfortunately there's just not enough room at the top for everyone to get an A. The only way to score big is to outdo everyone else. This section will show you how to make your paper stand up and be recognized by the professor.

What parts of your paper make the biggest impression on your professor? "Of course, the beginning and end," you say. Absolutely correct. You must grab the professor's attention with your title and opening. He's probably already read a load of papers, and by the time he reaches yours everything he sees just blends together in a big mush. Your title literally has to grab his attention and arouse his curiosity. Don't give it all away in the title - suggest, but do not reveal the contents of your paper. The average student gives no attention to the title, which results in a run of the mill impression, which ultimately creates a run of the mill grade. Don't be shy about coming up with something interesting. One tactic I used successfully was to create a title like a National Enquirer headline - seriously! For an analysis of Kafka's Metamorphosis, my title was "MAN MORPHS INTO HUGE DUNG BEETLE........RIGHT BEFORE HIS FAMILY'S EYES!!!" The title page was complete with a big ol' picture of a roach attacking a village or something. What do you think: did that catch the professor's attention? Of course, you have to make sure your professor has a sense of humor before you use this stunt. The essence is to catch your professor's attention in a way that won't offend him. Get the idea?

Rule #61 Use your paper's title to grab your professor's attention and arouse his curiosity.

OK, on to your introduction. First, never label it as an introduction. It comes first, so naturally it introduces the topic. If you've followed the procedure I advocate so far, the body of your paper is now excellent. Our objective is to create an introduction that will lead the professor into the body paragraphs with interest. You're pretty much on your own here, since the appropriate introduction depends so much on the topic. A formula that has always worked well for me is to start off with a very general perspective on your subject to show where your topic fits in and why what you have to say is important. Use only about three sentences to move naturally from general overview to a very specific problem - the question that you plan to answer. Then state your thesis. Rewrite your introduction as many times as it takes to get it right.

The last impression your professor has of your paper before he assigns a grade is your conclusion. Once again, never write "Conclusion" or "In summary..." Aim for a hell of a finish. Bring all of your evidence together and shock the prof with how cleverly you put it together. Amaze him with your insight into the problem! Save your best for the last, and rewrite it until it really shines. We're talking about your grade here, so take this seriously. Nothing is more important than your finish.

Rule #62 Your professor's last impression before he assigns a grade is your conclusion. Save the best for last.

Finally, go the extra mile to make certain the appearance of your paper is absolutely top notch. Never turn in anything handwritten! Learn to type or get a voice recognition system. Take full advantage of all the technology available to you. Use color scanners and printers if graphics or photos will aid your cause. Use a word processing program to spell check and polish the overall appearance of the paper and a quality printer to make sure the final product looks good. Bind your paper in a nice clear plastic cover. In short, make it look like a professional million dollar presentation. Your paper needs every possible advantage over its competition, so be creative!

Rule #63 An A paper always has a smooth professional appearance.

■ *Writing Style*

Here are a few notes on writing style to help you produce better papers. First, the average college paper's paragraphs are too long. Convey only one major thought per paragraph. Start the paragraph with your topic sentence describing what the paragraph will show. Every sentence that follows must contribute directly to the topic sentence. The final sentence of the paragraph establishes a transition to the next paragraph. Simple, right? Follow the formula. No twelve page paragraphs, much less sentences, unless your name is William Faulkner.

Rule #64 Every paragraph conveys a single thought.

Second, vary sentence and paragraph length (within reason) to create a more readable style. Use different types of sentences as well. One short declarative sentence after another gets very boring. If you don't know what I mean by different types of sentences, pick up a basic grammar book. You could definitely use the review.

**Rule #65 Variety in structure makes your paper
easier to read and more pleasing to the eye.**

Third, pick the simpler of two equivalent words when you have the choice. Professors typically aren't impressed by lots of showy vocabulary when simpler words convey the same meaning more efficiently. Why? Because their tired eyes have to read too much extra nonsense if you try to prove how many big words you know. Of course, if only a showy word happens to convey your meaning precisely, by all means use it.

Rule #66 Simplicity and clarity make the grade

Fourth, make very liberal use of illustrations, comparisons, analogies, metaphors, and examples. They're fun to read, hold the reader's interest, and show the professor that you understand not just what, but why. Your illustrations and comparisons to other fields of knowledge will show that you have an uncommon breadth of understanding, and also lend a very effective concreteness to your work. You can make any statement more concrete by adding modifiers. For example, you wouldn't say "This is a great book Darrin wrote." You would say, "Wow! I learned 140 different rules to increase my grade in any college course!" The idea is not to tell the reader how you feel, but to give him tons of concrete reasons why you feel the way you do. End result: the reader feels the same way you do. That means you get an A.

**Rule #67 Concrete examples, illustrations and
analogies strengthen your paper and
make it more interesting to read.**

■ Power Tips

I'm now going to tell you two of the most effective techniques you can use to score an A on an important paper. These two tactics worked for me more times than I can count, and surprisingly, I never saw another student in any of my classes use either of them. The first strategy is really only common sense, but the second one is more sophisticated and potentially dangerous to your grade if used unwisely. Used correctly, however, the second skill is more powerful than anything else I've shown you so far. Interested? Good! Let's get to it.

First, never think of writing a paper without pulling out a copy of a large book of quotations. This strategy applies to any paper in any class. *Bartlett's* is the best place to start. *Peter's Quotations* is also good to use if you're looking for something more modern or witty. The strategy is to read every single quote that deals with your topic, and see how you can apply the ideas to your course. A good quote is insightful, specific, interesting, and debatable. Hmm, do those qualities ring a bell? Sounds kind of like a thesis. Quotations are the best source I know of for a wide selection of potential theses for your paper. Copy all the quotes regarding your topic that you find interesting. Play with the ideas: combine them, reverse them, apply them to the lectures your professor has given. Adjust the ideas to make them specific, researchable, and debatable. Pick the idea that speaks the most to you, that you think you could prove convincingly. Now you have a direction for your paper - a thesis. Don't use the exact words of any quote without giving credit to the originator unless you like being called a plagiarist and flunking your class. Make the idea your own by stating it in your own words and adjusting it to fit your purpose. You've now successfully taken some piece of the wisdom of the ages and distilled it into a thesis for your paper. Not a bad start for a good paper, wouldn't you agree?

Rule #68 Consult a book of quotations for thesis ideas.

Another use of this same technique is to find a new approach when you encounter a block in writing or problem solving. Let's say you've tried everything you can think of to solve some difficulty in your paper or on a homework assignment, but you continually come up empty handed. What can you do? My favorite ploy in this situation is to open the nearest book to a random page. I point my finger anywhere on the page, read a sentence or two, and see if I can come up with some way of relating what I've just read to my problem. Does that sound strange to you? It works because our minds have an amazing way of associating all sorts of seemingly unrelated concepts in meaningful and creative ways. Try it a few times before you pass judgment. If you're stuck anyway, you've nothing to lose.

**Rule #69 When you're stuck, open a random book
and relate what you read to your problem.**

I've known a few people who would criticize this next tactic as somehow dishonest, but in actuality it's part of a very important exercise that cuts to the very heart of a college education. College may be described as four year's worth of trying on for size the ideas of others. You keep the ideas you like, discard the ones that don't have meaning for your life, and in the end hopefully emerge a more enlightened individual with a much broader experience of the way the rest of the world thinks. Part of the process of deciding which ideas suit you personally is looking for confirmation that the ideas are valid. The final tactic is excellent practice.

Here's the idea: adopt temporarily the stance regarding your topic that your professor holds. Look for something specific that your professor feels very strongly about. Herein lies the power of the technique: prove your professor's opinion in a new and interesting way that he's never conceived by himself. Beware, though. If you can't come up with something new, your professor will just think you're an intellectual butt kisser and have no respect for you. Create an original and convincing argument, and your professor will think you're the single smartest person he's ever encountered (with the exception of himself, of course). Why? Because you not only share his view, but also used a clever argument to prove it to be more reasonable than any alternative! In doing so, you vindicate his belief and gain his respect. His assigning you an A on the paper and in the class is a matter of course. In the process, you've had the extremely valuable experience of stepping into someone else's belief system and learning how it works. Not only do you get the grade, but you learn a valuable lesson you can use for the rest of your life. Additional effective ways of handling your professor follow in the next chapter.

There were a total of eighteen rules introduced in this chapter. Record your ranking here:

1. _____

_____

2. _____

_____

3. _____

_____

4. _____

_____

5. _____

_____

6. _____

_____

7. _____

_____

8. _____

_____

9. _____

_____

10. _____

_____

11. _____

_____

12. _____

_____

13. _____

_____

14. _____

_____

15. _____

_____

16. _____

_____

17. _____

_____

18. _____

_____

DEALING WITH YOUR PROFESSOR

6 What motivates your professor? With very few exceptions, your professors hold their positions because they have devoted many years of their lives to learning, understanding, and researching their subjects. As a result of their effort and years of study, they have become experts in their fields and deserve your respect. Most professors have a need for recognition of their work. The typical professor feels that he's an important person, and on some level he gets off on the fact that he is the authority. Lucky for you, very few students ever express a sincere admiration and respect for a professor's accomplishments. Your professor wants to be consulted as an authority on his subject. You can show your respect for your professor by doing exactly that: asking for his help. If you follow the seven steps of this chapter, both you and your professor will be better off. You'll have a much greater understanding of his subject, and he'll have the satisfaction of having done his job well.

■ *Prepare Before You Talk to Your Professor*

The first step is preparation to talk to your professor. At some point you're going to need to see your professor during his office hours or before class to ask a question. The single most important thing you can do is clarify the issue that you want to see him about in your own head before you open your mouth. Describe in writing for yourself exactly what you hope to gain from talking to your professor. Organize your thoughts, write down the questions that you want to ask him, and then use one of the memorization techniques in the next chapter to commit the order of everything you want to talk about to memory. Why are these techniques valuable? First, thinking in advance about what you want to discuss helps you think more clearly about the issues. Second, your organization will show your professor that you're a serious student and that you respect his time. Finally, you'll give the impression of having a highly uncommon clarity of mind.

Rule #70 Organize your thoughts and questions in writing before you see your professor.

■ *Visit Your Professor After Tests*

The second technique is to pay your professor a visit after any test, especially if you made a low grade. First we'll deal with the case of a low score on the test. Use the low grade as a signal that you're off course in your studies and your understanding of the subject. Tell your professor you feel you're off course and that your score on the test demonstrates that fact. Say that you find the subject very interesting, and that you would value his input on the measures you could take to regain your footing. Any professor will provide a few pieces of advice here - it's his job to teach you the subject, after all. Your objective is for him to take a personal interest in your success in the class.

Rule #71 Get your professor to take a personal interest in your education by asking his advice.

When you leave his office, give thought to your professor's recommendations and put them to use. With your effort, your professor's advice, and the aid of the techniques in this book, your grades are certain to improve. When you make progress, be absolutely certain he's aware of it by paying him another visit to thank him again for his assistance. You've just given him partial credit for your success, so he'll begin to take further responsibility for your results. He will not want to see you fail, because he'll take it personally. In effect, you become something of a protégé.

If your grade was already high, take a trip to the professor's office to confirm the few points you missed. You gain an understanding of the things that confused you, and your professor associates your face with your high grade. You already begin to construct a favorable image in your professor's eyes.

■ Research Your Professor

The third step is virtually unknown among undergraduate students. Your professor is highly unlikely to hold a position at any halfway decent college without having published at least some research in an academic journal. Use the library's database for his discipline to find a list of his works, or ask the department secretary. Find a copy of the journal and read what he published. It may be way over your head, but just try to get a general idea of what problem he was addressing from the abstract at the beginning of the article and the conclusion at the end. Write down the points that he makes and find a way to apply them at some time to what you're doing in his class. When you get the opportunity to relate one of his points to what is discussed in class, ask him a question about it and his image of you will soar. He loves his subject and feels important because of the contribution he made with his publication. When you show him that you read and understood (at least in part) his work, you acknowledge his importance in a way that he has probably never experienced in one of his classes, and demonstrate that you're a serious student who deserves an A.

**Rule #72 Learn the primary distinctions and
findings of your professor's research.**

■ *Keep Up with Current Research in the Field*

The next step is closely related to the third. Every few months, take a brief look at the academic journals. See if any of the papers published there relate to the topics you're studying in class by reading the titles and abstracts. The whole process will only take a few minutes per journal. If any of the papers relate to your class, read them the way you did your professor's works. Take special note of the ideas presented in the papers and make every effort to apply the current research to your class. You'll learn things well beyond what the other students are learning, and your professor will be immeasurably impressed. Very, very few students demonstrate this much interest in a subject. Remember that your professor loves his subject (usually). If you take a few minutes to show extraordinary interest in the topics to which he devotes his life, you score major points.

Rule #73 Learn what problems academics in your subject are currently working on.

■ Be Aware of Current Events

The fifth step is to pay attention to what's happening in the world by reading newspapers and magazines. Your study of many subjects such as history, government, economics, psychology and the natural sciences can be greatly enhanced by bringing a knowledge of current events into your classroom. The professor will think he has done a fantastic job educating you if you can apply what you learn to what you observe happening in the real world. Bringing up related outside information in the classroom shows the professor that you're well-informed and that you think about his subject even when you're not in class. You enrich the classroom experience for other students while you build a favorable image with the professor. Everybody wins.

■ *Act with Enthusiasm*

Step six relates to how you conduct yourself in class. Most students sit around in class waiting to be told what to do. When they're finally told, they grumble under their breath about how unfair the professor is, how unrealistic his expectations are, how it will be impossible to complete the assignment by that date, etc. You know exactly what I'm talking about - you've probably done it yourself! What you need to remember is that the classroom is not a democracy by any stretch of the imagination. Sure, you can convince some professors who have all the authority and strength of a wet noodle to change their minds, but the vast majority only resent the attempt to subvert and challenge their decisions. If you want to argue about the rules in the class and the unfairness of the "system," you can choose to prove you're right, or you can choose to win the game by making an A, but you usually can't do both. What's more important to you? When you're asked to do something or given an assignment, attack it with all your enthusiasm and energy! If you sit around whining, you just waste your energy being pitiful. Take initiative, be creative, and do your best regardless of whether or not you like the rules.

**Rule #74 Time spent complaining is wasted.
Use your time enthusiastically to complete all
assignments you're given.**

■ Praise the Good Ones

Finally, every one of you has had or will have truly outstanding professors in college. Some profs have a true gift for teaching their subjects that comes from a love for their life's work and a commitment to showing students what they regard to be beautiful and worthy of study. Do you remember a teacher that brought a subject alive for you? If so, take a few minutes and write an unsolicited letter to the chairman of the department describing the value of the educational experience you received in the professor's class. Every campus has teaching awards. Nominate your favorite professor for an award. Your professor never has to know you wrote the letters or nominated him - you don't do something like this to brown nose. Do it because you value what you learned thanks to your professor. You owe him that much at least.

**Rule #75 Give credit where credit's due:
recognize the good professors.**

One last point: never use any of these techniques insincerely. If you do, your professor will know immediately, and his image of you will suffer as a consequence. Never attempt to make an impression on someone by faking. Everyone will see through you, and nobody likes a brown noser.

**Rule #76 Honesty isn't the best policy –
it's the only policy.**

There were a total of seven rules introduced in this chapter. Record your ranking here:

1. _____

   _____

2. _____

   _____

3. _____

   _____

4. _____

   _____

5. _____

   _____

6. _____

   _____

7. _____

   _____

IMPROVING YOUR MEMORY

7 This chapter contains an explanation of how your memory works and a description of the techniques you can use to improve it. For some reason, many people who regard themselves as sophisticated college educated individuals look down on techniques to improve memory as dishonest tricks. Professors scorn memorizing information because they say college is for "learning how to think." However, the plain fact of the matter is that you will improve your grade in any and every class you take by increasing your capacity to recall information when you need it. The only way to have tremendous amounts of relevant facts at your fingertips is to memorize them. This chapter will show you how to do so as efficiently as possible. I used these techniques continually to dumbfound my professors and fellow students. If you practice and use them, your friends will swear you must have a photographic memory, and your grades will begin to increase immediately.

■ What is Memory?

Do you have a bad memory or a good memory? Either answer - you're wrong! OK, it's a trick question. Memory is not something that you "have" because memory is not a thing. Memory is a process. If you think you have a bad memory, all that really means is that you don't currently understand how to learn and remember information effectively. Remembering well is a learned skill, not an innate ability.

Rule #77 Memory isn't a "thing." It's a learned skill.

It's just like everything else: if you want to do it well, you must learn the principles, apply them, and practice. You can't simply read this chapter and suddenly have a photographic memory. I will show you the techniques to improve your memory process, however the techniques don't necessarily make everything easy. Memorizing is hard work, but I can show you how to do it more quickly and more efficiently than you ever thought possible.

**Rule #78 If you want to master any skill,
you must learn the principles, apply them
when appropriate, and practice.**

■ The Three Stages of the Memory Process

If you desire to remember something, you must take three steps. First, you have to acquire the information. It's a little hard to remember what you don't learn in the first place! Second, you have to store the information in your mind in a way that makes it easy to access. Finally, you have to retrieve the information you stored whenever you happen to need it. If you "forgot" a piece of information, then something went wrong with one or more of those three steps. This section of the chapter will describe ways you can improve each of these three steps.

■ Information Acquisition

Senses

Meet the three S's of information acquisition: Senses, Spaced Learning, and Sleep. What is your dominant learning sense? Do you understand and remember best what you hear? What you see? What you feel? Only you can answer this question for yourself. Are you more likely to remember information in your textbook, or something that your professor says? Can you take your VCR apart and then remember how to reassemble it? Figure out which of your senses helps you remember most effectively. You can be in real trouble if you don't know that your primary learning sense is kinesthetic (touch) or visual, and you find yourself in a class with nothing but lectures - no text, no overhead projector, no laboratory. You may fail to acquire the information altogether, so you have no hope of remembering it.

**Rule #79 Discover which sense you
use most during learning.**

Once you discover your best learning sense, you can restructure your learning experience to suit your needs. If you're a visual learner, summarize the information to be learned in interesting visual patterns on the page. One strategy of this sort that I made use of was for remembering to which group a particular piece of information belonged. Consider a history course about the French Revolution. It's essential to remember the political associations of the different players in this historical drama, so I listed the members of the Jacobins, Girondists, the Mountain, Feulliants, and the Cordeliers all separately in their own parts of the page. I drew a landscape with a mountain, a jack-o-lantern, a giraffe, a fire, and some clouds. On the mountain I wrote the names of the members of the

Mountain, the Jacobins in the jack-o-lantern, etc. All I had to do to remember who was a member of what group was to recall visually on what part of the page I had written the name. You can also use this technique to great effect in a foreign language class. In your French or Spanish class, if you keep a list of irregular verbs on the top right hand side of the page, and regular ones on the bottom left, all you have to remember is where on the page the verb is located in order to recall how to conjugate it. Experiment with this strategy and find new ways to make it work for you.

**Rule #80 Restructure your learning experience
to concentrate on your dominant learning sense.**

If you're an auditory learner, summarize the information you need to remember, record it in your own voice, and then listen to the tape a few times. Make up a little song if you have musical talent (or even if you don't). Learning researchers in Eastern Europe claim to have produced some fantastic results by orally introducing new pieces of information every eight to ten seconds while students relax and breathe in rhythm with music. They say classical music with a pace of sixty beats per minute is optimal for learning. I personally have never tried their methods, but they're worth a shot. They're supposed to be able to learn entire languages in only a few weeks!

Finally, if you learn best when you have something physical to touch - something with substance and structure, you can still tailor your classwork to fit your mode. Build a structural outline of the material you need to learn. Think about the interconnections that bind the topics together. Now cut up the outline into pieces with only one fact per piece. Alternatively you could use an individual notecard for each fact. Shuffle all the pieces and then rebuild the structure from memory of how everything fits together. You'll find your grasp of the subject to be far superior to what it would have been had you only tried to read or listen to the material.

Regardless of which sense you use the most, try using all of these methods to appeal to all of your senses for maximum recall. The more ways you learn something, the more likely you are to remember it.

Rule #81 When learning, use as many senses as possible to give yourself more ways to remember.

Spaced Learning

Let's say you can afford to devote a total of three hours to studying a certain subject over the course of a week. What do you think would be the most effective allocation of your time if you want to maximize how much you learn? I found through a great deal of experimentation that I remember best when I break the three hours into four segments of forty minutes a piece, and space them out over the course of the week. I used the remaining twenty minutes in five minute increments within an hour of the session to do a quick review of what I had learned. After a week, I could remember at least twice as much information as if I had spent the entire three hours in one single session. This study plan worked very well for me throughout college, so I used it without investigating why it works.

Recently I looked up some research by psychologists to discover if they had the same results with the subjects of their controlled studies. Their scientific studies produced results similar to my own. They found that two hours of study could be made most effective by dividing it into four thirty minute sessions spaced over a few days. The reasoning behind the increased recall was that if we attempt to continue to learn beyond the duration of our attention spans, the new information interferes with what we have already learned, clouding everything new and old alike. If you take a break or give yourself something entirely new to think about (something dissimilar enough that it won't be confused with what you just learned), your mind has a chance to consolidate the new information

---

before anything else can interfere with it. The end result is that spaced learning reduces the total amount of time required for any learning task.

Rule #82 For effective study and maximum recall, space your study sessions over time.

So here's the strategy for you to take from this section: study a single subject to the limit of your attention span, then take a five minute break to move around a bit and get something to eat. Then attack a totally different subject with renewed vigor, pausing for a few minutes later on to review the first subject. Adjust the plan in whatever way you find most appealing. You may have an exceptionally long attention span, or you may just really get involved in a subject and not want to stop after forty minutes. Do what feels right for you.

Sleep

Remember what that is? If you're like most college students you have a vague memory of what it used to be like to sleep once in a while! Well, I'm here to tell you that sleep is great for remembering things. How's that? Sleeping on a subject (going to sleep right after you study something) improves how well you remember what you learned. Once again, psychologically speaking, your mind has a better chance to consolidate what you have learned if you give it time off from thinking. On a related note, you remember worst what you learn right after you wake up.

I'm a huge advocate of naps. My favorite way to learn has always been to take thirty to forty minutes after class to review in detail everything I learned, then drift off into dreamland for a little while. Somebody would wake me up and say, "What are you doing sleeping?" I'd answer, "Shut up and leave me alone! I'm consolidating what I just learned!" Try that one

---

next time your professor rudely interrupts your naptime! Just kidding, of course. Standard disclaimer here: WARNING: Sleeping during class has been found to contribute directly to the impairment of the acquisition stage of learning and recall.

So, what have you learned in this section? You remember the most if you sleep right after you learn. How are you going to use that to your advantage? A little post-learning nap during the day is great if you can manage it. Don't forget to study before you go to sleep the night before a test. And by the way, don't forget to actually go to sleep the night before a test, OK? Good deal. Naptime, everybody!

**Rule #83 Sleep after you study to remember
more of what you learn.**

■ *Storage*

Organization

Two similar groups of students were independently given the same collection of information. The first group was told to learn the material as thoroughly as possible in a specific period of time. The second group was given the same amount of time and told that their task was simply to take the information and organize it. How much better do you think the first group remembered the information? Twice as well, you say? Three times? Guess again. Both groups recalled the information equally well. Are you surprised? The more you consciously organize material the first time you encounter it, the easier it will be to recall later.

**Rule #84 You remember best what
you organize in advance.**

Think of the process of efficient information storage as the act of putting everything you learn in a large mental filing cabinet. The usual way a student stores information is to throw everything together in a great big random pile. If that's how you store information in your mind, I bet you answered the first question of this chapter "I have a BAD memory!" It's much easier to retrieve a piece of information from memory if you organize everything you learn in advance and know exactly where to place the information in your mind. Would you rather try to find something that you filed in a logical manner, or something that you cast into a pile of junk? Every popular memory technique is simply a way to organize information before you learn it.

What steps can you take to organize before you learn? Well, the first step is to carry out the preview as described in the reading skills chapter. Previewing the material you're about to learn puts everything in perspective - it prepares your mental filing cabinet to receive information by creating and opening the appropriate files before you even start to read. Another way to organize in advance is to write down a goal describing exactly what you intend to learn during a particular study session. A whole collection of information organizing techniques is described in the last part of this chapter.

Association

If your memory process is like a filing cabinet, the easiest way to set up the system to allow you to find a piece of information is to cross reference it in as many other files as possible. Association is the tool you can use to learn new information very effectively. Anytime you learn something new and unfamiliar that you think is important to remember, associate it in any way possible with other facts and ideas that you know well and are very comfortable with. Find ways to relate it to many different subjects. The more references you create for the new information, the more likely you are to learn, understand, and remember it.

Rule #85 Associate new information with facts you already know to enhance understanding and recall.

Make your associations with the new information span all the different senses. Let's say you're attempting to remember a new vocabulary word. First associate it visually with other words you know. What other words are spelled in a fashion similar to the new word? What words is the new one made up from? Second, associate the pronunciation of the word with other words. What words does the new one sound like? What does saying the word feel like in your throat and mouth? Associate the new piece of information with as many senses as you can, and you give yourself more ways to remember it.

Imagery

The human mind can store and remember images very well. The simple act of including pictures in a book increases recall of the text. One reason for this effect is that the act of creating or viewing an image stores the information in a second part of the mind. Instead of just using verbal memory, you access visual memory as well. You have twice as many links to the information in your mind, so your ability to recall is improved. Most sophisticated memory techniques (like the ones discussed later in this chapter) make very heavy use of visual imagery to store information.

Rule #86 Create an interesting image whenever you want to remember.

Context

Context is defined as the total environment in which you learn a particular fact. Your mind has an interesting way of anchoring what you learn to certain cues from the context. Have you ever tried to remember something you read, but didn't succeed so you grabbed the book and flipped it open and then suddenly remembered before you looked it up? This occurrence is quite common. The reason you remembered when you opened the book is that you recreated a context similar to the one in which you originally learned the information. The implication for effective storage of information you learn for easy recall is to use a variety of interesting and different contexts when you learn different subjects. The more contexts you use, the more environmental anchors your mind has to link up with the new information. Lighting, posture, mood, furniture, sounds, and even the color of ink and paper you use all contribute to the context. If you're having difficulty remembering something important, try either to recreate the context in which you learned it or imagine the context as vividly as possible.

One very effective study method I often used in college was to prepare for a test in the same classroom in which the test was to be held. I would wait to study until the classroom was empty, then review my notes and memorize whatever facts I thought I would need during the test. When test time came, the context was automatically recreated and remembering everything was easier. Try for yourself and your grades will confirm it.

Rule #87 Jump start your memory by recreating or vividly imagining the context in which you learned.

■ *Retrieval*

Overlearning

One way you can make retrieval of stored information much easier and faster is to overlearn the material. Overlearning is defined as learning beyond the point of mere recall. Let's say you spend an hour learning something like the bones of the human body. After one hour you successfully recite for the first time all the information you needed to learn. If you continue to study the same material for another fifteen minutes, you will remember a great deal more of the information than you would if you stopped as soon as you succeeded once. You will learn the information more thoroughly, you will be able to recall it more quickly, and you will have much greater confidence in a testing situation.

Rule #88 Overlearn for fast and accurate recall under pressure.

Review and Feedback

Another way to improve your ability to retrieve information from memory is to actively practice retrieval and give yourself feedback on how well you're doing. The first step is to recite as you learn. Remember our discussion on recitation back in Chapter 2? If not, read it again and then recite it. Recitation is simply practicing retrieval. If you don't retrieve the information well enough when you recite, you know that you need to go back and store the information better.

If you want to learn something so that you remember it over the long term, the surest way is to review the information at increasing intervals. First, review and recite anything you learn within one hour after the learning session. This rule applies to all learning: reading, lecture, study, etc. Spend a few minutes reviewing again the next day, then again within a week, again after three weeks. You will eventually own the information permanently. One informal study found that students exposed to the same pieces of information on six consecutive days remembered thirty times as much after two weeks as students who were exposed only one time.

Rule #89 Review important information at increasing intervals to impress it upon long term memory.

Think Around It

Let's say you're taking a test, and one important fact escapes your memory. You've tried everything, but you still draw a blank. Try this final key to better retrieval: think around whatever you're trying to recall. Give a few moments' thought to everything imaginable that you associate in any way with what you're trying to remember. Your mind has several links by which it can access the information you're trying to retrieve. If one of these is temporarily blocked, thinking around it will help you find other links to the same information.

■ *Memory Techniques: Mnemonics*

So far we've talked about how your memory works and discussed a few ways that you can improve the acquisition, storage and retrieval stages of the memory process. The six techniques that follow all specialize in improving the storage process. Some of the strategies date back at least 2500 years. These are the most powerful mental information storage and retrieval methods known to man.

Acrostics and Acronyms

I'm sure you're already familiar with these two devices. An acrostic takes the first letter in each word from a sequence of words and substitutes another, easier to remember word that begins with the same letter. For example, the order of operations in math can be remembered by the acrostic Bless My Dear Aunt Sally (Brackets, Multiplication, Division, Addition, Subtraction).

An acronym is an easy to remember word constructed from the first letter of each word in a sequence. For example, HOMES represents the Great Lakes (Huron, Ontario, Michigan, Erie, Superior). Both of these devices are simple, easy to use and effective. Anytime you need to remember a short sequence or the members of a certain group, make up a little acrostic or acronym. I used an acronym memorization technique very successfully in college. If the test had essay questions, I would first use my notes to predict the most likely questions. I would then work out an outline of what my answer would be for each question. Finally, I would summarize each point I wanted to make in a single word, then make an acronym out of the first letters of each of those words. I would memorize my acronyms right before the test, then write them down on the back of the test as soon as I received it. This technique gives you a huge head start on your competition because you can almost always predict one or more of the questions. Find which ones you have already prepared for, look up your acronym for that question, fill in the words that make your outline, and except for the details, you're done. The other students will still be trying to figure out what to write.

**Rule #90 Use acrostics and acronyms to
remember short lists of items.**

Keyword Mnemonic

This technique is especially well suited to learning new vocabulary, whether foreign or your native tongue. The essence of the technique is to construct a concrete, easy to remember keyword from the spelling or the sound of the word you want to learn. First we'll do an example from English. Let's say you want to learn and remember the meaning of the word gregarious, which means sociable. Take the second syllable, gar. Visualize a huge twelve foot long alligator gar with a big adhesive name tag that says, "Hi! My name is Greg." Instead of eating other fish as most gar are fond of doing, Greg is a friendly fish who likes to swim around and talk to his neighbor fish. Can you visualize this? I mean really see it. Once you see this image and reinforce it a few times, you will never be able to forget the meaning of gregarious, even if you want to!

Now let's do a Spanish word: biblioteca, or library. The last two syllables sound like "take a," and the first two are spelled like Bible. See a Spanish librarian standing at the door of the library offering a Bible to all of the patrons who enter:"Bible, take a Bible for your reading pleasure. Thou shalt not talk in the library." Now do you think you'd remember what biblioteca means? These two examples are just things I made up with no real effort. I'm certain you can come up with much more imaginative and meaningful images of your own. The key is actually to see the image in your mind's eye, and to incorporate some sort of interaction between the parts of the image. The beauty of this technique is that it doesn't really require much effort, but it is very effective!

**Rule #91 Use the keyword mnemonic to quickly
master foreign and native vocabulary.**

The Link Method

This system is very effective for remembering a sequence of information. The first step is to form a concrete visual image for each item to be remembered just like you did in the keyword mnemonic discussed above. Next, visualize an interaction between the image representing the first piece of information and the image representing the second piece of information. Condition the interaction by visualizing it repeatedly and vividly. Proceed in the same way for the rest of the list: link the second image to the third, the third to the fourth, etc. until you reach the end of the list. Whenever you create the association between the images, use the first one that comes to mind. Associate the first item in the list with some cue that will be present when you need to remember the sequence, your professor for example. Your cue will provide the starting point, and if your associations were visualized well enough, the rest of the sequence will follow quickly and easily.

I have a few tips for you that will make this method more effective. First, any items you see in a visualization should interact for maximum recall. Motion and exaggeration are much more memorable than a static image. Don't just think about the interaction - close your eyes and actually see it. Imagine the colors and outlines of all the items. Bizarre images may be more memorable for you simply because they require more time and effort to formulate. Actual pictures work even better than visualization. Try drawing a few pictures to help you remember your images. Use whatever works best for you.

Rule #92 Interaction, motion and exaggeration increase your imagery recall.

My two favorite uses for this technique are remembering a lecture without taking notes and memorizing a long sequence of events for a history class. If you listen actively and think during a lecture, you can actually achieve better recall and understanding than someone who takes lots of notes and reviews them later. Professors' lectures are usually, but not always, fairly well organized treatments of a particular topic. To remember the lecture, the first step is to grasp the main points that the professor makes. A student recording every word spoken doesn't have an opportunity to stop, think, and find the main ideas. Once the professor makes an important point, form an image to represent the point in your mind. Be creative and make it memorable. Amuse yourself! You may be the only person who is actually having fun. When the professor makes his next point, construct another image and link the two with some sort of interaction. Proceed through the entire lecture, reinforcing your images and links with repetition as you go. When the lecture is finished, you'll have greater understanding and recall than the students who act like stenographers.

A history class is really just one huge exercise in linking. Historians even like to help you out with the links by proposing cause and effect relationships. Link everything in your course together in a meaningful, memorable way and you will achieve an incredibly powerful command of the subject. History professors like nothing more than a student who can propose a theory to explain a certain course of events and back it up with proof. If you skillfully link together the sequence of events in your memory, you will be able to recall many, many times the amount of relevant proof for the essay questions on the tests as the other students. As you might have guessed, you'll get the grade. Try out the link system in your classes. Give it a chance before you pass judgment.

**Rule #93 Use the link method to memorize a lecture
or a long list of information.**

The Loci System

Greek and Roman orators commonly used this method to remember their speeches. It's still around today, so you know it's effective. Here's the story. Select a route that you frequently walk and know well. When I was in college, I liked to use a walk across campus. At a school like the University of Texas at Austin, home to 50,000 students, that's quite a walk. Visualize in order the different buildings you pass. You need a set of ten to twenty individual locations. Now let's say you need to remember a sequence of fifteen facts. Take the first piece of information, construct a concrete image to represent it in your mind, and link it to the first location on your walk. Repeat for the other items in the sequence. When you need to remember, take a mental walk through your locations and pick up the item you linked to each of them. Locations you're familiar with are extremely easy to visualize, so your linking is already half complete before you even start. That's the power of this method.

**Rule #94 Use the loci method to remember a speech
or any long list of items.**

If you'd like to use this system to remember items for several classes, I'd suggest you follow my simple procedure. Use a different set of loci for each class. I used the buildings I would pass on the way to the class I was studying. This method has two advantages. First, using a different set of loci for each class prevents interference from different subjects. Second, you can review literally by walking to class. Why waste the time you spend walking across campus? Use this method and you can look at the buildings while you walk, reviewing the links you have made and strengthening your memory!

One final use of this method is to cure simple forgetfulness. Have you ever had something you need to remember to do later pop into your head? Sure, and you think, "Oh, I need to make sure I don't forget to do that!" Of course, you forget when the time comes, and then kick yourself later. A very easy way to solve that problem is to take the item you need to remember and link it very strongly with the location or person you will see when you need to remember the task to perform. For example, if you need to remember when you get home to call the guy who's repairing your car, form an image of the mechanic hanging from your living room ceiling by the phone cord. Gruesome and disturbing? Well, maybe. Memorable, and flashes into your mind when you get home? Yes! Now you'll remember to make that call.

**Rule #95 Use the loci method to
cure simple forgetfulness.**

The Peg System

This system is very similar to the loci system, but instead of locations you use a set of prememorized concrete nouns that correspond to numbers. For each item in sequence that you need to remember, link it to the corresponding concrete noun:

1. gun	6. sticks
2. shoe	7. heaven
3. tree	8. gate
4. door	9. wine
5. knives	10. hen

Feel free to adjust these concrete nouns to suit your purposes, and to create a longer list if you need it. You can pick whatever you like, but just make certain the nouns you pick correspond in some way to the number they represent. One way to create a list of nouns four times as long is to modify each one with a season of the year. Imagine the first ten concrete nouns associated with winter, the second ten with spring, the third ten with summer, and the last ten with fall.

Use this system just like the loci system: link the information you need to remember to the concrete nouns. The advantage of this system is that the link also provides you with the number the piece of information represents in the sequence. For example, if you were to memorize the Presidents of the USA in sequence using the loci system, and someone asked you who the twentieth president was, you'd have to go through your entire sequence of locations counting out the numbers. With the peg system, all you'd have to do is think of the noun you use to represent the number twenty, then remember what you linked to that noun. In the system described above, the noun for the number twenty is a hen in the spring. Can't you see Garfield (the cat) sniffing a nice fresh spring flower as he dines on Jon's Cornish Hen? If so, you'd remember very easily that James Garfield was the twentieth president. If you see Jon finally slaughtering his pesty pet, you might also recall that Garfield was assassinated. Get it?

Rule #96 Use the peg system when you need to remember not only a list, but also the number of each item in the list.

I used this system frequently to prepare for open book tests. Time is always the challenge during an open book test. Anybody could get all the answers given enough time and enough books. I used the peg system to remember in which book and in which chapter I could find the information I needed. I would just summarize the information in each chapter, and then link a keyword to the concrete noun associated with the book number and chapter number. Blazing fast!

**Rule #97 Prepare for an open book test
with the peg system.**

Number to Sound System

The 350 year old number to sound system is by far the most sophisticated and powerful memory method described in this book. If you have the need to remember many numbers, or if you need to remember a sequence of information larger than the peg system can handle, this is the answer. Be forewarned: this technique requires time and quite a bit of practice to master. Once mastered, however, it will enable you to remember more information than any of the other systems.

The number to sound system assigns a consonant sound to each of the numbers between 0 and 9:

1. t, th, d   6. j, sh, ch, soft g

2. n   7. k, q, hard c, hard g

3. m   8. f, v

4. r   9. p, b

5.   10. z, s, soft c

Vowel sounds and the consonant sound h are free - you can use them anytime without having them represent a number. The essence of the system is that you can assign a word to any number imaginable. If you need to remember a phone number: 867-5309, you would represent it as f-soft g-k-l-m-s-p. What could you make this say? How about fudge climbs

---

a pie? Remember everything is phonetic. The only two consonant sounds in fudge are f and soft g. Even though d is in the spelling, you can't hear it so it doesn't get a number. Climbs has k, l, and m - you can't hear the b so it doesn't count. A pie has only one consonant sound: p. Do you understand how this system works? Try it out with your phone number. Now you understand the first use of the number to sound system: remembering numbers.

The second use is an elaboration on the peg system. Instead of using a hen in the spring to represent the number 20, you would use n-z to represent the digits 2-0. Nose would make a good concrete noun. There's no limit to high you can go with the number to sound system. You could conceivably recall a list of 10,000 items if you wanted to do so. Memorizing the Periodic Table is a piece of cake when you learn how to use this system quickly.

**Rule #98 Use the number to sound system to
remember numbers or very large lists of information.**

■ *Practice and Use These Systems!*

Now you have access to six powerful memorization systems. I've given you tons of examples of ways to use these techniques in all sorts of different classes. It's now up to you to find an application for what you have learned in this chapter. Don't move any further in this book until you find something you would like to have memorized. Maybe you'd like to know all the steps to effective reading from Chapter 2. Perhaps you want to memorize the steps of the process of homebrewing beer. Maybe the numbers of every player on the football team. It really doesn't matter what you want to memorize, just that you'd like to have the information available instantly whenever you want it. Decide which of the methods in this chapter is most appropriate for your information, then do it. Prove to yourself how effective these methods are. Discover that you really can memorize and remember what you learn!

There were a total of twenty-three rules introduced in this chapter. Record your ranking here:

1. _____
   _____

2. _____
   _____

3. _____
   _____

4. _____
   _____

5. _____
   _____

6. _____
   _____

7. _____
   _____

8. _____
   _____

9. _____
   _____

10. _____
    _____

11. _____
    _____

12. _____

_____

13. _____

_____

14. _____

_____

15. _____

_____

16. _____

_____

17. _____

_____

18. _____

_____

19. _____

_____

20. _____

_____

21. _____

_____

22. _____

_____

23. _____

_____

STUDYING FOR MAXIMUM RESULTS

8 The chapters on reading skills and memory methods have provided you with a tremendous number of powerful techniques to increase the effectiveness of the time you spend studying. Knowing the techniques is one thing, but using them for greatest effect is entirely another. This chapter will show you how to create the best physical and mental environment to take full advantage of the skills you've learned so far.

■ *Your Learning Context*

Remember the section of the previous chapter that explained the importance of the context in which you learn? If not, take a minute or two to review it now. The best way to study for any class is to duplicate the external conditions which you will experience when you need to recall the information you're studying. In most cases, we're talking about a classroom where you'll take a test. Use this context as a guideline for determining where you should study. During the test: will there be music in the background? Will there be a television blaring? Will your friends stop by to visit? Will you be lying on a nice comfortable bed with a big fluffy pillow under your head? The answers to these questions demonstrate what sort of study environment you must find. It should be very clear to you that if you want to make your study time really count, you shouldn't even try to do any studying in your dorm room or apartment. The best environment I know of is an empty classroom. If for any reason a classroom isn't available, pick the most isolated spot in the library. Admit no distractions while you study if you want to have more free time and better grades.

Rule #99 Duplicate during study the external conditions you will find yourself in when you need to remember.

■ *Your State*

Have you ever had a really hard time studying? Nothing went right, you couldn't concentrate, and you couldn't understand the subject? It's happened to all of us. Can you think of a time when your study experience went well? Everything clicked and made perfect sense? Suddenly you could see the big picture and feel exactly how everything fit together? I'm sure you have. The only difference between these two experiences was your state at the time you were studying. You were the same person during both study sessions, but in the second case you somehow managed to get yourself into a very powerful, resourceful state. Your were able to focus your attention like a laser beam and penetrate the subject.

According to practitioners of Eastern philosophies of self control as well as researchers of Western sciences such as psychology, your state at any given time is determined by the way you use your body and your mind. This section will teach you how to take conscious control of your mind and body to produce the most effective state for study. There's nothing mystical about any of these techniques - they're just common sense ways to help you gain focus and improve the results of your study time.

**Rule #100 The effectiveness of your study session
is determined by your state, which in turn is a result
of the way you're using your mind and body.**

■ *Your Body*

The first step is to get comfortable, but not too comfortable. You need to study, not sleep. Pick a sitting position, clothing, and lighting condition that you like. Think back again to that perfect study time you've experienced sometime in your past. What was your posture at that moment? Were you sitting up perfectly straight or were you hunched over? Reconstruct the way you were using your body at the time that everything made sense to you. How were you breathing: deep, even breaths from your abdomen, or quick shallow gasps from your lungs? Were your muscles tired? full of energy? tense? relaxed? How would your body feel if you were completely centered and concentrating on your studying? Complete Exercise Seven in the back of your course to determine the essence of how you used your body. Now duplicate those conditions. It doesn't matter whether or not your body feels like doing this - just pretend for a few minutes and you'll soon feel like studying. Try this procedure and you'll be a believer. When you recreate your state, you recreate your result.

Rule #101 You can put yourself into an effective state for study by changing the way you use your body.

The time of day you select to study also plays a part in determining how effective your study session will be. Everyone's body goes through certain cycles during the day. At some times we're more able to concentrate and think than at others. When is your most centered, alert part of the day? Plan your most difficult study sessions for your most powerful times. Don't let society's norms dictate when you schedule classes and when you study. If you're a night person, schedule your classes in the late afternoon and use the evenings to get your work done. Sleep all morning if you like. If you are most effective in the mornings, get up at 5 or 6 a.m. to give yourself a few hours of work time before classes. Just know your body and use your best hours (no matter when they fall) to tackle your most difficult tasks.

**Rule #102 Use your most productive hours
for your most difficult tasks.**

Of course, frequently we all have to study at times when our bodies and minds don't exactly want to work. If you have difficulty staying awake while you study, leave some sort of assignment that requires writing for those times when you feel most sleepy. It's very easy to fall asleep when you're reading or reviewing notes, but not so easy if you select an activity that involves physical effort and motion such as typing or writing. Just plain old common sense. Another way to stay alert is to get up and move around. Raising your body temperature helps your mind stay awake. Take a break every fifteen or twenty minutes if you have to. Stretch your muscles, do some jumping jacks or pushups. One very important "stretch" that most students forget to do is to shift the focus of their vision to something distant at least four times an hour. This practice helps you combat eye strain and headaches from too much reading.

**Rule #103 If you have difficulty staying awake, try
some homework that requires you to write or type.**

■ Your Mind

Let's examine that ideal study session from your past again. What were you thinking? How did you feel about the subject you were studying? How did you feel about your ability to understand the material? What was it like to be completely focused? Complete Exercise Eight to get to know how you use your mind. Generate all of these feelings and thoughts again, but this time see yourself experiencing all of these feelings while you tackle the task in front of you now. Rekindle these feelings anytime you sit down to study. Once again, recreate the state and you recreate the result. The results you get when you study are a direct reflection of what you project mentally. If you think the subject is a ridiculous, uninteresting waste of time, then your results will mirror your attitude. If instead you find something interesting to concentrate on, see the value of the material and feel your ability to master it, then you'll succeed.

Rule #104 The results you get when you study are a direct result of the thoughts you project.

Do you think you're doomed as a student because you have an extremely short attention span and just can't manage to concentrate for any length of time? Pardon my harshness, but if you think that, you're full of crap! With a few extremely rare medical exceptions, everyone has the ability to concentrate for a sufficient amount of time to study effectively. You can choose to make excuses for yourself, or you can choose to get things done. Which will it be?

What do you enjoy doing with your spare time? Do you like to watch sports? Play sports? Listen to your favorite CDs? Shop for hours looking for just the right outfit at the right price? Play computer games or chat on IRC? OK, now what's the approximate duration of your recreation? An average football game is three hours (or longer). Most CDs are around an hour in duration. I've seen girls shop from 8 a.m. until 10 p.m.!! When you're having fun, do you have to stop your mind from wandering from your entertainment so you can concentrate on having fun? Of course not! You concentrate for the entire period, sometimes for hours, without even thinking about it. The point here is simple enough: every single one of you has the ability to concentrate on the things that interest you. Period.

Rule #105 If you're interested, you can concentrate.

Now that you know that you definitely have the ability to concentrate, let's talk about how you can carry that over into your studying. Recreate the feeling of rapt attention and interest you have when you're doing what you love to do. Imagine yourself interested and focused. Can you capture the feeling? Now start studying, and pretend that you're interested in the same way. It may seem silly, but believe it or not, you can cultivate concentration by pretending to be interested even if you're not. For at least fifteen minutes, refuse to let your mind wander. Direct any stray thoughts gently back to your studying.

**Rule #106 Sincerely pretend that you're interested
for a few minutes, and you will have
the ability to concentrate.**

There's a tremendous advantage to developing strength of focus. Remember how I told you that I was able to take an above average honors course load, participate in varsity athletics for three hours a day, hold down a part time job, have a girlfriend, and still ace every class? Concentration and absolute focus made that possible. If you can keep all your energy and thoughts on the task in front of you, you greatly shorten the amount of time necessary to complete it. You can do only one thing well at a time, so concentrate completely on your goal and give it everything you have. The result will be better grades and more free time to do what you enjoy.

Rule #107 Absolute focus is the key to accomplishing a great deal in a short period of time.

As a finish to this section, here's a great little concentration technique from yoga to help you center on your task. When your mind wanders, pause for a moment and look for an object with an interesting but simple outline. I like to use a picture frame or clock. Trace the outline of the object with your eyes, moving as smoothly as possible along the entire outline. Continue tracing the border for about a minute, centering all of your thoughts on the object. Now that your thoughts are more focused, move back to your studying.

■ Dynamics of a Good Study Session

There are three parts to an effective study session: objective, procedure, and reward. This section shows how to design a study session to help you achieve the most in the shortest period of time. As a quick reminder, return to the previous chapter and review the section on spaced learning to make sure you understand how to put several study sessions together into an effective whole.

Objective

Know exactly what you want to achieve anytime you sit down to study. Make your objective explicit by writing it down. Once you have your written objective, don't give in to any distraction until you have achieved your goal.. Simple enough, right? Now start doing it every time you study. It was always helpful for me to give my goal a time limit and then work against the clock to finish quickly. Depending on your personality, this may or may not work for you. Give it a try and find out.

Rule #108 Express in writing exactly what you hope to achieve every study session.

Procedure

Effective learning of any subject occurs in four stages. First, preview and organize the material so you know exactly what you're getting into. Next, concentrate and read the information you need to learn. Third, recite the information to make sure you understand it. Fourth, use the information you learned to solve some sort of problem. You may also want to use a memory technique to memorize the material for quick recall. Another aid to learning is to talk to yourself continually as you work. Tell yourself the goal you're trying to reach, and how you're going to achieve it. This simple act will improve your focus on the task at hand. That, in a nutshell, is the most effective study procedure I have ever encountered.

Once you finish a study session, follow it with a test session to see how well you understand and remember the information you studied. Quiz yourself. Be harder on yourself than you expect the professor to be, and your real tests will be a breeze. The process of self testing provides you with incredibly valuable feedback on how well you're doing. If you haven't tested what you've learned, you haven't really studied.

Rule #109 Alternate test and study sessions to obtain feedback on your progress.

Here's one final tip for studying and learning that I discovered by accident. I did a great deal of tutoring during college. Other students in my classes frequently would approach me for help, so since I'm such a nice guy I would set aside an hour or so a week to help each one of them. In reviewing the basics with them, I found that the foundation of my own understanding was so strengthened by overlearning that I could reduce my study time for tests by more than half and still pull the same grade! The tutoring sessions actually helped me at least as much as the other students. I learned that if you really want to understand something, put it into words and explain it to someone who doesn't understand. You know what else? Word eventually got around that I was helping sometimes as much as a third of the class to improve their understanding of the subject. What do you think that did to my professor's image of me as a student who deserved an A?

Rule #110 Explain what you know to someone else and you truly understand.

Reward

We all work better if someone dangles the appropriate carrot in front of us. What's your carrot? What potential reward would spur you on to a stronger effort? If you think about it, the automatic rewards for doing well in school are numerous. Maybe they're already sufficient motivation for you to give school your all. However, not everybody thinks far enough ahead to be motivated to work at this very moment when something more immediately appealing (like a party) beckons. If you frequently procrastinate and/or lack motivation, practice a little self discipline. Take an activity that you'd really like to do, and tell yourself that you won't allow yourself to do it until you complete some important assignment. Use leisure time as a reward for attaining the objective you set for yourself at the beginning of the study session. If you enforce your decision, you'll gain a new respect for your ability to achieve, and you'll also get to enjoy your free time without any guilt whatsoever.

Rule #111 Use leisure time activities as a reward for accomplishing your study goals.

There were a total of thirteen rules introduced in this chapter. Record your ranking here:

1. _____
   _____

2. _____
   _____

3. _____
   _____

4. _____
   _____

5. _____
   _____

6. _____
   _____

7. _____
   _____

8. _____
   _____

9. _____
   _____

10. _____
    _____

11. _____
    _____

12. _____

_____

13. _____

_____

PREPARING FOR TESTS

9 Many students complain that tests are so unfair, or so biased, or hampers to real learning, or irrelevant, etc. You know what I say? I don't say anything. While the other students were complaining, I was too busy either preparing for the test or having fun because I had already finished preparing. You can whine about tests if you like, but you're only wasting time, breath and energy. Tests are a part of life, so accept them as they are and make the most of them. If you think about it, you'll realize that they're actually pretty good for you. What besides a test can motivate you to such resourceful efforts at gaining knowledge? How else can you determine if you've really mastered a subject and are ready to move on? At their best, tests accomplish these two things better than any other educational tool. Tests are your friends!

■ Consistent Actions

I've already suggested a couple of actions to perform consistently throughout the semester that will help to prepare you for any test. First, you're supposed to be concentrating on the main ideas the professor presents in every lecture, then making an outline of those ideas every day after class. Remember that? Every week, take a few minutes to perform this extremely valuable exercise for each class: organize the week's main ideas into an outline, then review the outlines for every week so far. These outlines should be very concise. No more than one page per week per class. Get an idea of where the class has taken you and where it's headed. Build the transitions between the main ideas and get a feel for the overall structure of the class. Reviewing these notes every week will greatly ease the burden of cramming for a test. Since you're reviewing the information at intervals during the semester, you're committing it to long term memory.

Rule #112 Create a main idea outline for each class every week. Review the all of your outlines for the entire semester at the end of every week.

Second, you're also supposed to be a test question detective all semester long. Make special note of anything your professor emphasizes. Think of all the most likely and toughest test questions imaginable. Add them to the last page of your notebook. Don't let a single class day go by without making a contribution to your list of questions. Ideally you'll think of several possible questions every time you do a reading for class or attend a lecture. These questions are a gold mine. Sometimes I've managed to prepare in advance for every question that ended up on the test. Talk about an easy A!

Rule #113 Constantly be on the lookout for potential test questions.

■ *Preparing for a Specific Test*

The actions above will help you prepare for all tests during the course of the semester. Here are four more actions to help you prepare for any specific test.

Know What to Expect

If your professor has taught this class before, do anything ethically within your power to get your hands on copies of old tests. Sometimes professors put them on reserve for you in the library. If not, check with the club for that particular major, like the Psychology Club or the Economics Club, to see if they maintain a test bank. Frats often have fantastic test banks dating backs years. If you have to, ask your professor directly for a copy of his old tests. The worst that can happen is he'll just say no. Just be resourceful. It's good for you - builds character.

Rule #114 Obtain copies of your professor's tests from previous years.

Don't rely too much on the old tests though. Professors have been known to throw some pretty good curves. They'll change one word in a question that will alter its entire meaning. If you're not careful, you won't even be answering the right question. Use the tests primarily as an indicator of structure and types of questions.

■ *The Essay Test*

Four types of tests are most common. Your preparation is highly dependent on the type of test. The first type, and the most common in the majority of college courses, is the essay test. A good answer to the typical essay question requires a mastery of general overall principles and a vision of the big picture. This fact is especially applicable to final exams that span an entire semester. If your professor is fond of these type questions, be especially careful to recognize any general statements he makes during class, and more importantly, the specific details he offers to confirm his assertions. When he does this in lecture, he is answering his own essay questions in advance. One powerful strategy for essay tests is to memorize verbatim a few good quotes that you could apply to a variety of different questions. If under test conditions you manage to back up your answer with an appropriate quote from an authority on the subject, you're well ahead of your competition.

Rule #115 Memorize several good quotes that you can apply to a variety of questions.

■ *The Objective Test*

The second type of test is the run of the mill objective test. There are a slew of old wives' tales about how to pick the right answer to a multiple choice or true/false question if you don't know it already. These strategies are virtually worthless in a college class. Your professor may or may not create tests to which these tactics may be successfully applied. Instead of concentrating your effort on learning schemes to guess the right answer, why not instead spend your time preparing so you actually know the right answers? Objective tests usually concentrate on details as a matter of practicality. You can't exactly deal with the meaning of life on a multiple choice question: "Complete the following sentence with the best answer of those given. The meaning of life is..." Yeah, right. Proper preparation for an objective test is to glance over general principles as a framework, then concentrate on the details. Memorize everything you can, but focus your efforts on your professor's favorite topics. He's more likely to ask about those.

Rule #116 Concentrate on the details to prepare for an objective test.

■ The Problem Test

The third type of test is the problem test common to physical and mathematical sciences. These tests are usually very straightforward: the professor states a few problems and you have to solve them. "So, tell me something I don't already know," you say. OK, I will. Problem tests are greatly simplified by the fact that there are only a few types of problems covered on any test. All you have to do to prepare is to look back through all of your homework, list every type of problem you've had to work since your last test, and enumerate a step by step methodology for solving each type. Be on the lookout for problem types that combine several smaller types of problems into a big one. Sadistic professors just love those! Memorize the methodology for each type, then test your ability to solve problems under time pressure by making up a few problems of each type and working them out as quickly as possible. Simple as PI .

**Rule #117 Memorize the methodologies for solving
every type of problem you'll encounter.**

■ The Open Book Test

Fourth are open book tests. These may be a combination of any of the above types of tests, but they differ in that you're allowed to bring in notes or books. Piece of cake, right? Not usually. First, the questions are usually harder than regular test questions. Second, the test is usually longer than a regular test. If you hope to be able to look up the answers as you go along, you're in real trouble. I recommend two techniques to prepare for these tests. Treat the test just like a closed book test. Prepare for it the same way you would if it covered the same material with the same type of questions, but you only have access to what you bring into the classroom inside your head. Next, use the peg or number to sound memory system to memorize the basic contents of each chapter of each book you get to take into the test. If you need to look up something, you'll know instantly where to look. Take these two steps to prepare for an open book test, and while other students are leafing through their books in a desperate attempt to finish the test, you'll be checking over your completed test a second time just to make sure you answered everything correctly.

**Rule #118 Prepare for an open book test just
as you would for a closed book one.**

■ *Mine Your Gold!*

Remember how I said that your potential test question collection is a gold mine? Now it's time to mine it! Take all the questions relevant to the material the test covers and formulate your answers in writing. If it's a math or science test, solve the problems or develop the proofs. If it's an essay test, outline your answers. If it's a junior high style objective test with true/false and multiple choice questions, concentrate on all the small details necessary to answer the questions of your small-minded lazy professor.

**Rule #119 Formulate answers to your semester's
test question collection.**

■ Practice

It's not enough just to answer the questions you've formulated. You need to practice answering them until the answers are second nature. Practice is the mother of skill! You may know the answers now, but we want to make certain you'll know them when it counts. Here are the steps to ensure you will perform under fire:

First, practice the answers to your questions in a no pressure environment until you are very comfortable with all of the material. Spend an hour or two a day for four or five days before the test. You should be very confident that you can handle anything thrown at you.

Second, try to duplicate the pressure and time limits you'll face in the actual test situation. If the test is a performance of a musical piece or a speech, get yourself an audience and practice in a variety of different contexts so nothing can surprise you. If it's a regular test, go to a classroom and set up a timer. Take a mock test. Let the pressure of the event serve as a signal to attack aggressively. Take this step on the last two days before the test.

Rule #120 Practice your answers to the questions first in a no pressure environment, then under test conditions.

Finally, keep the entire event in the proper perspective. It's not life or death. If you've prepared yourself as I advocate, you're ready. Just relax, cast away all cares and be confident that you can handle it.

■ Study Group

If you can find a few other like-minded serious students, get together with them one night a couple of days before the test and ask each other the questions that you've saved up all semester. Everyone should have his ten best questions ready to ask the other students. This can be an extremely valuable experience. Each student has a different perspective, and exposing yourself to as many perspectives as possible will do more to prepare you for what your professor may ask than your perspective alone. Be warned though. Lots of students waste too much time when they get together for a study group. If the students you work with are more concerned with BSing than with preparing for the test, don't waste your time. Associate with people who have a positive attitude about their education and are willing to put forth the effort to make the grade. Maybe you can find someone else who has read this book!

**Rule #121 Use the different perspectives of other
students to prepare yourself for the test.**

■ *Study Schedule*

Combining all of these preparation tactics, we arrive at a six day schedule for study:

T-6: Review all of your notes and main idea outlines for the semester.

T-5: Formulate answers to your potential test questions.

T-4: Review main idea outlines again, practice answering your questions.

T-3: Practice answering your questions, meet with study group.

T-2: Practice answering questions of the other students.

T-1: Review notes, practice under test conditions. Relax.

Feel free to adjust this schedule to meet your needs. Your test may be more difficult and call for more preparation, or it may be a breeze. Do what works for you.

■ Developing Confidence

There are two types of strategies for developing confidence. One type consists of all the things you can do before a test to get ready, and the other type is composed of the tactics you can use while you're under fire. We discuss the first type here. Strategies for use when you're actually in the test will be dealt with in the next chapter.

The primary emotional enemy of confidence before the test is worry. Worry has to be the biggest and most ridiculous waste of energy ever conceived. If you spend a minute worrying, how has your plight changed? Well, you did absolutely nothing during the course of that minute to prepare yourself for the test you're worried about, and to make things worse, that minute you just wasted is gone forever. So, your test is one minute closer and you're no better prepared. Now you have even more reason to worry! Sounds really stupid, doesn't it? Unless you enjoy making yourself feel bad and wasting time, decide right now that worry is a poison of which you'll never partake again. It simply doesn't do you any good.

If you begin to feel worry about some future obstacle, acknowledge it as a signal that you need to take action immediately to prepare yourself. Your only point of power to change things is the present. This book is full of ways to prepare yourself and kill worry, but you have to take action. Practice, overlearning, and effective test taking skills give you all the confidence you'll need for any test.

**Rule #122 Acknowledge worry as a signal to take
immediate action to prepare yourself.**

The second biggest enemy of confidence is regret over some past mistake. You may generalize some bad result on a test to mean that you're stupid or that you will never be able to understand that subject, but criticizing yourself for a past mistake and passing judgment only harms you further. Concentrate instead on learning everything you can from your mistake, then banish it from your thoughts forever. Your performance in the future will not be determined by your past. It will be determined by the actions you take now to prepare yourself. If you wish to dwell on something from your past, find some empowering successful result you've created and think about that.

Never fear making a mistake - everybody makes them while learning. Accept them as friendly indicators of the things you need to put more effort into learning. Don't take them as gauges of your worth or intelligence. Learn from them and forget them. Think only of the goals you have before you.

**Rule #123 Mistakes are invitations to learn more.
Once you take value from the mistake and learn how
to correct it, dismiss it from your memory.**

There were a total of twelve rules introduced in this chapter. Record your ranking here:

1. _____

_____

2. _____

_____

3. _____

_____

4. _____

_____

5. _____

_____

6. _____

_____

7. _____

_____

8. _____

_____

9. _____

_____

10. _____

_____

11. _____

_____

12. _____

_____

MAKING THE GRADE ON TESTS

10 Want to make an A? Well, you have to learn how to take tests like a real pro. I've aced more tests than I can count with the aid of the techniques in this chapter. Read on to learn how you can do the same.

■ *The Day of the Test*

The ideal start for test day is sleep. If you feel the need to pull an all nighter, you may as well throw in the towel now because the fat lady already sang her song for you. Use the techniques in this book to prepare yourself starting about five or six days in advance, and you'll sleep very well the night before the test. Review your lecture notes and your potential test questions one last time, then go to sleep.

What you eat the day of the test is more important than you think. "Oh, I know this one! Eat a big, full breakfast the morning of the test. I learned the four food groups!" If that's what you say, what you're about to learn is worth far more than the price of this book. Why is it that you're not supposed to swim until an hour after you eat? Because your body directs most of the blood you have to your digestive system to pull nutrients out of the food, and when you require all the blood for another activity like swimming, you get bad stomach cramps, right? Because of all the energy it requires, digesting a big meal just makes you want to curl up in a warm bed and take a nice, long nap. Now, I'll be the first to say that naps are great, but not right in the middle of a test! Your mind and your body other than your digestive system require a substantial blood flow when you're taking a test. Your blood should be upstairs carrying oxygen and nutrients to your brain and your writing arm during a test, not downstairs helping digest steak and eggs. It doesn't make any sense at all to burden your body with the task of digesting when you'll need your energy for thinking and writing.

So what's the answer? Fruit! Nature's greatest food source provides you with all the nutrition you need without burdening your body. Fruit doesn't require much energy to digest, so unlike a heavy breakfast, it provides you with energy during a test rather than stealing it from you. Try eating light before a test. Just fruit in the morning, maybe some hot veggies, salad and some kind of bread for lunch if your test is later in the day. Give your body a chance to get used to this strategy before test day. Don't just suddenly turn your diet around 180 degrees the day of the test.

Rule #124 Eat light before a test - preferably fruit.

Another good strategy before the test is to get a little exercise. Mild exercise will do a couple of beneficial things for you. First, it allows you to release some of that test day tension that builds up as the time draws near. You can just let your mind relax while you focus on the monotony of good jog. You'll feel refreshed and ready to go when you're finished. Second, exercise raises the body temperature a little above normal. A small increase in temperature has been shown to increase mental efficiency. Give it a try and see if it works for you like it does for me. Take the same advice as for diet, though. If you don't ordinarily exercise, don't just suddenly try it two hours before a test! Make it a regular habit - it's good for you!

Rule #125 Exercise before your test.

Finally, prepare all of the materials you will need for the test in advance. Avoid a last minute scramble to find your calculator and pencil before you sprint across campus to get to your test five minutes late. That's not exactly what I had in mind when I said a little exercise before a test is a good idea. You may totally lose your composure if you have to rush. Get everything ready way early and arrive on time. Sit up close so you don't have far to go in order to ask your professor a question.

**Rule #126 Prepare your materials in advance
and get to the test on time.**

■ *Dealing with Test Anxiety*

Let's say you've prepared yourself for this test and you really know your stuff. You've even practiced it in a simulated test environment like I recommended in the last chapter. But no matter what you do, you freeze up when the professor puts the test in front of you. Your mind draws nothing but a blank. Has that ever happened to you? If so, I'm going to help you make sure it never happens again. First we'll talk about changing the way you use your body, and then I'll give you a few strategies about how you use your mind.

■ *No Tight, No Fright!*

Scientists have proven that it is literally impossible to feel anxiety when your body is relaxed. If you have no tension in your muscles, you simply cannot be afraid or anxious. The answer is clear, isn't it? All you have to do is relax your body. Tons of books give you techniques to relax, so feel free to consult them if you want to try relaxation methods different from what I'm going to tell you. The procedure I use (a very common one) is to relax muscles in sequence going up my body from my feet to the top of my head, one muscle group at a time. I simply contract the muscle I'm concentrating on for a few seconds, then release and feel the tension drift away. I like to visualize a nice, warm bright light engulfing me and flowing into my lungs with each measured, deep breath. A couple of minutes worth of controlled breathing from deep in the abdomen coupled with this muscular relaxation technique does wonders for me. If you ever draw a blank when you see the test, take just two little minutes and relax your body.

Rule #127 Relax your body and anxiety disappears.

Once you're relaxed, ask yourself, "How would I be sitting right now if I knew all of these answers? What would it feel like to be completely acing this test?" Now, assume the position. No, not that one - the position you imagine yourself being in if you're really doing well on the test. Don't dismiss this as nonsense. Look around some time at students taking a test. You should definitely be able to tell who is doing well and who is desperate by posture, breathing and facial expressions. Assuming the physical characteristics of someone who knows what he's doing actually helps you do better, believe it or not. Listen to me here - I've made more A's than anyone else you know, and I'm not any smarter than you are! I just know how to make A's. Or if you'd prefer the advice of William James, heed what he wrote:"You do not sing because you are happy - you are happy because you sing."

■ What are You Thinking?

The cause of any anxiety you feel is the way you think about the test situation. A circumstance has meaning for you only because you assign a particular meaning to it. Is failing out of college bad? Well, that all depends on how you look at the situation. It may be bad if you assign a tremendous value to a college education. But what if you think the school of life is where you truly learn, and flunking out of college will allow you to get on with "real" life? Depending on your outlook, you could view the same situation with regret or rejoicing. What happens is not important - only what you decide it means to you matters.

Rule #128 As Epictetus said, "Men are not afraid of things, but of how they view them."

Tests are not an inherently scary event. Being chased by a very hungry 1500 pound grizzly, now that qualifies as scary in my mind! A test isn't going to shred you with its claws and then eat you. As a matter of fact, if that's the criterion for scary, then the test should fear you. Think about it - you can shred the test and eat it if you like, correct? If tests cause you anxiety, it's only because you attach a lot of emotional baggage to the possibility of receiving a bad grade. "There is nothing either good or bad, but thinking makes it so." Change the way you think about grades, and you eliminate your anxiety.

What stigma do you attach to a low grade that makes it bad? Does a low grade mean that you're an idiot or a failure? Does it mean that you're incapable of learning anything? Of course not! A low grade simply means that you didn't take the proper actions to win the grade game. That's really all there is to it. A low grade doesn't suggest anything at all about you as a person. It just means you didn't produce the result you

---

desired. A low grade is actually very valuable. It tells you that you've taken the wrong course and that you need to adjust so that you can learn what you need to know. It's a meaningful and useful signpost on the road of life. Given that a low grade doesn't have any implication for your worth as a person, is a test any reason to get scared?

Rule #129 A low grade only means that you need to change your actions in order to win the grade game.

You can think of a test as an opportunity to prove what you know, or perhaps as a game giving you the chance to discover how good you are. Those would both be advantageous ways to see a situation that you'll be facing whether or not you like it. Unfortunately most students see a test as a crisis situation. Let's look at the situation in that light and see how bad things really are. There are only two possible outcomes of the test crisis. What happens if you fail the test? Does the college bump you back a year? Do you somehow know less than you did before the test? Of course not. At the very worst, if you fail a test you stay exactly where you are. Well, I guess you could get kicked out, but you can still transfer your credits to another school and stay at roughly the same level. So the worst that can happen is that you don't make any forward progress.

What's the best possible outcome of a test crisis? You win big, make an A+, and impress the hell out of everyone you know! Will the test situation be something completely different from anything you've ever experienced? Of course not! The test will present nothing new whatsoever. You've been through it 1000 times before, and this test is no different. It's definitely not life and death. The range of outcomes can be anywhere from standing still to making a huge leap forward in your education. So what's so bad about a crisis like that? What do you have to fear?

**Rule #130 A test is an opportunity either to stand
still or to make progress.**

OK, you've done everything possible to think your way out of anxiety. Now I'll give you a way of feeling your way out. Remember the exercise we did in the chapter on effective study where we called up from memory a time in your past when you had great success studying? Now we're going to do the same thing with a test from your past. Recall your greatest success on a test. Recreate that past event again and feel it. What were you thinking? Were you confident or scared? Did the answers just pop out of your mind with complete ease? Did you feel as if your entire body of knowledge flowed through you onto the test paper? Complete Exercise Nine now. Conjure the feeling of success that you felt at that very moment. Now visualize yourself completing the test you feel anxious about. Bring your feelings of success into your visualization. When the feeling is strong enough, you become so resourceful that you can do no wrong. Now you're ready to take your test. Reread this section anytime you face a test that makes you anxious.

**Rule #131 When the feeling of inevitable success is
strong enough, you can do no wrong.**

■ Test Taking Skills

The entire approach to test taking is just common sense. The problem that most students have is that common sense becomes very uncommon when they're under pressure. There are six simple steps to taking any test. Memorize the steps using linking or an acronym so you'll always have them in mind when you're taking a test. Commit this common sense to memory and you'll own it forever.

Neatness

Not much effort is required to make your test the neatest, best organized one in the class. Remember, everything is sales, and the appearance of your test is very important. If your answers are well organized and easy to read, your professor will have the impression that the test was a breeze for you. In addition, you will make his job of grading easier and your grade will reflect it.

Rule #132 Neatness and organization help you distance yourself from your competition on tests.

What steps do you think you could take to make your test look better without taking up much of your test time? How about erasable ink or pencil rather than a regular pen? If you constantly have to mark through parts of answers to change them, your test will be very difficult to read. You may have the correct answers, but your professor won't be able to find them. If your professor has to work to find your answers, your grade will suffer.

Planning and organization help as well. If your test has short answer or essay questions, outline your answers in advance so that you'll have a structure to follow when you write. This tactic will prevent you from rambling aimlessly.

If your test is composed of problems, draw a box around every answer to each part of the question. Simply pointing out your solution can save your professor several minutes of wading through all the steps you took to arrive at the answer.

Preview

Read through the entire test before you begin answering questions. Pay complete attention to the directions. You need an idea of what you face so you can plan the best use of your time. Allot time to each question according to its point value. For example, a question that counts for 25% of your grade deserves 25% of your available time. Be sure to save the last 10 minutes of the test to review your answers. Write down the clock time you need to begin each question or section and keep to your schedule.

Rule #133 Preview the entire test and assign times to each part before you begin.

On essay or problem tests, very briefly outline the approach you will take to answer the hardest questions on a piece of scratch paper before you start the test. This technique will allow your mind to begin working on the answers subconsciously. When you think of some additional part of the answer, take a moment to stop what you're doing and jot it down under your outline so you don't forget.

Another good reason to read through the test in advance is that you may detect a connection between the questions. Perhaps one of the questions contains the answer to another question, or maybe all of the questions are intended to lead you toward the answer of the last and most important question. Unless you preview, it will be too late when you discover the relationship.

Talk to Yourself

Silently, of course! Scientists have learned that your task accomplishment behavior is more effective if you consciously give yourself instructions. "I have plenty of time. I'll read the directions carefully to make sure I understand the question. I'll preview the entire test, plan how to use my time, and keep my answers neat." You get the idea. Avoid at all costs any negative talk. Don't discourage yourself. Just give yourself instructions on how to do everything correctly.

**Rule #134 Give yourself instructions mentally
as you take the test.**

Answer What You Can, Abandon the Rest

Answer the easiest questions first. Your best use of time is to get down on paper everything that you know for certain to be correct. You maximize your grade and build confidence for the harder problems to come. By the time you hit the hard ones, you'll have a full head of steam and be used to getting the answers. Attack the hard problems aggressively!

**Rule #135 First finish all of the questions to which
you're certain you know the answers.**

If you hit a block that you can't seem to break through, abandon the search, mark the question, and return to it last. There's no sense in banging your head against the wall when you still have other questions to answer. You'll only frustrate yourself and endanger your ability to finish the rest of the test with a cool head. Plus, there's a pretty good chance some part of the answer will pop into your head later if you just relax.

**Rule #136 Skip any problem that is giving
you too much trouble.**

Objective tests are straightforward. You either know the answer or you don't. Be careful not to read anything into the problem and out think yourself. If you don't know the answer, the only thing you can do is eliminate the choices you know are wrong then flip a coin.

Problem tests are also straightforward in the results you must produce, but the method is up to you. The best procedure I know is first to rewrite the problem for greater understanding. Next, write down every given piece of information you can use to solve the problem. With the givens and the desired result in front of you, you should be able to recognize the type of problem from your list of types you created to prepare for the test. If not, break the problem into smaller and smaller pieces until you reach a level of simple problems that you recognize. Now all you have to do is recall the solution methodology you memorized and apply it. Once the smaller parts are solved, rebuild the large problem one piece at a time.

**Rule #137 Break any hard problem down into
smaller pieces until you reach something you can solve.**

Essay tests are usually straightforward neither in the result desired nor the reasoning you must use to arrive at your conclusion. The best tactic for an essay test question is to rewrite the question, state your thesis up front, then back it up with as many important, concrete pieces of proof as you have time to write. Try for three or four detailed, specific and concise body paragraphs - one for each individual piece of proof. Make each paragraph reasonably short and well organized. The more relevant facts you can bring to bear, the better. Beware filling up the page with BS, though, unless you think making an F is your optimal outcome.

Go Back and Try Again

If time allows, now is your chance to return to the questions you abandoned. First see if your mind has provided you with the answer while you weren't paying attention. Try to answer the question again. Think all the way around the question - try to associate it with something else you know. If you still draw a blank, don't worry. You're certain to remember it right after you turn in your test! Just give it your best guess and move on to the next step: a final review.

Review

If you find that you've run out of time, use the last ten minutes to submit a rough outline for any essay questions or problems you were unable to reach. Tell the professor what path you were planning to take to reach a solution. Give him some reason to award you partial credit. A blank answer is worth absolutely nothing, but a decent outline could get you half credit or better. If you've run out of time on an objective test, use the last few minutes to madly fill in any answer you like. Never leave anything blank (unless your professor uses a grading system that penalizes wrong answers like the SAT).

**Rule #138 If you were not able to finish,
use the last ten minutes to submit outlines
for problems you were unable to reach.
Never leave anything blank.**

If you have finished the test with time to spare, use all the rest of the available test time to reread the questions and review your answers. Are you certain you answered the questions asked? Sometimes you might answer the question you like rather than the question asked. It's better to discover that fact now when you have a few minutes left rather than have your professor discover it for you. Also, it's not uncommon for additional useful information to occur to you when you review, so incorporate it into your answers.

Last thing to check when time's up: did you put your name on the test?

■ *After the Test*

If you really want to learn the material, the most important part of the test is finding out what you don't know. Immediately after the test, look up any answers you couldn't remember. When you get the test back from your professor, correct everything you missed and add it to your notes as something to be reviewed weekly. You'll make the final exam so much easier by learning how to correct everything you missed.

Rule #139 Correct every test question you missed and record it in your notes.

Go see your professor in person after the test. Most professors determine grades on one or more of the following three criteria: progress, effort, and total knowledge. In the eyes of your professor, your test score reveals your total knowledge. You may be able to increase your grade in the class by appealing to your professor's sense of the other two criteria. Fight for a grade if you think you deserve it. The visit to your professor is especially important after the final exam. Go see him after he's determined grades for the semester, but before he submits them to the registrar. It's much easier to get a grade changed before the grades become official. If you're borderline, now's the time to assert yourself and be as persuasive as possible.

Rule #140 Fight for your grade before your professor submits it to the registrar.

There were a total of seventeen rules introduced in this chapter. Record your ranking here:

1. _____

_____

2. _____

_____

3. _____

_____

4. _____

_____

5. _____

_____

6. _____

_____

7. _____

_____

8. _____

_____

9. _____

_____

10. _____

_____

11. _____

_____

12. _____

_____

13. _____

_____

14. _____

_____

15. _____

_____

16. _____

_____

17. _____

_____

PLAYING THE GAME

11 So far we've talked about goals, reading skills, selecting classes and professors, listening and note taking, writing skills, dealing with professors, memory techniques, effective study, and test taking skills. We've covered just about every strategy that can help you improve your grades in college.

The content of the first ten chapters of this book has been shaped to a large degree by my particular understanding of college and the way it works. There are many different ways to think about education - many ways that are very different from my perspective. So that you know exactly where I'm coming from, I'm going to tell you the four basic axioms upon which my entire philosophy of grades is based. Try these principles out yourself. See if they make sense to you. If you find, as I have, that they're extremely useful for getting what you want out of college, apply them to the rest of your life as well.

■ The Ballpark Rule

College is a huge game, and grades are how you keep score. Before you play any game, you have to understand two things. First, you have to know the rules. Second, you have to live with the consequences of your decisions within the game. Many students don't succeed simply because they don't understand the rules. We've corrected that problem.

Now that you know the rules, you have to decide whether or not you want to play by them. The alternatives are to break them or try to change them. In my opinion, these options are both a waste of your time. The consequences of breaking the rules can be extremely costly: you can get thrown out of school and lose everything you've worked for. Trying to change the rules of this particular game is an exercise in futility. The only reasonable option is to play by the rules. Hence, the Ballpark Rule: (you may have heard the Golden Rule: He who has the gold makes the rules! This is my adaptation for college)

Axiom #1 The Ballpark Rule:
He who runs the Ballpark makes the Rules.
Either play by his Rules, or change Ballparks.

Your professor runs his own game. As long as his rules are within those accepted by the administration of your university, you have to play by those rules or change professors. The implication for your studies is, first of all, make a special effort to find a professor whose rules you like. That was the reasoning behind Chapter 3's discourse on taking your professor for a test drive. Second, play within the rules and use them to influence your professor in your favor - the motivation for Chapter 6 on how to handle your professor.

■ The Competition Rule

Grades are not primarily indicators of your intellectual potential nor are they gauges of how much you know. They are simply your score in the game. They tell how well you played against your competition: the other students.

Most professors grade on a curve. In other words, they assign grades on a competitive basis: actual test scores don't matter, only their relative rank among the scores of other students in the class. Many professors will attempt to make the distribution of grades in their classes resemble the Normal distribution from statistics. Why? Because they take too much heat from the administration if there are a lot of A's or F's. The Normal distribution, or Bell Curve as you may have heard it called, is safe for the professor because there are a few A's and F's, a few more B's and D's, and mostly C's. This rule is imposed by the administration on the professor. He may feel like giving everyone an A or failing the entire class, but if he does he won't be around for long.

What does this mean for you and your grades? You're in competition with a lot of students for only a few A's. Take full advantage of every opportunity to distinguish yourself and put distance between your professor's image of you and his image of the others. For example, if you complete every homework assignment accurately, neatly, and on time, you're a leg up on your competition. It's just common sense.

Axiom #2 The Competition Rule:
Your result will be determined by your standing
relative to the other students in the class.

■ Sales, Sales, Sales!

So you're in competition with everyone else for just a few A's, and you need to distinguish yourself. Now's the time to remember that everything is marketing. Everything you do in class: how you listen, what you say, how you treat others, everything you write in your homework and on tests, and everything you say to your professor during office hours all contribute to your professor's image of you. In the end, he'll decide based on your total image whether or not you deserve one of those A's. If you want the grade, you have to sell the professor on the idea that you deserve it. Doing well on tests is sometimes enough all by itself. If you don't quite make the grade on tests, use your comments in class, your homework, and your discussions with the professor to convince him that you're a serious student who's made a lot of progress and expended a great deal of effort on his class. He'll respect you and you'll have a very good shot at the grade.

Axiom #3 Everything is marketing!

■ *The Special Something That Will Distinguish You*

This is probably the most important idea in the entire book. Pay attention here! Once again, it's common sense that is so uncommonly put into practice. No matter what the situation in school: homework, readings, papers, tests - always deliver more than is required. If your professor wants you to have three outside sources for your paper, use five, and make them sources no one else will think of. If the term paper is due at the final exam, finish it, turn it in a week early and tell your professor, "Here's my paper. You can have it early so maybe your grading load will be a little easier next week." If your computer program is supposed to be able to handle three different input options, master those three and add another one that you think is equally important.

This philosophy of action can be applied to any situation you encounter. Anytime you have an assignment, ask yourself, "How can I go the extra mile here? What can I do to make my effort really stand out?" Remember the Competition Rule? You need to distinguish yourself from the competition, and going the extra mile achieves that goal beautifully. As Zig Ziglar wrote, the extra mile "is one stretch of highway where there are never any traffic jams." Consistently make the extra effort and you'll be all alone on top of the heap.

Axiom #4 Go the extra mile.

CONGRATULATIONS,
YOU GRADUATE! NOW WHAT?

12 You've used all of the techniques in this book to graduate with flying colors. Because of the relationships you were able to cultivate with a few professors, you have in your hand a diploma and some fantastic letters of recommendation. Thanks to your self searching goal setting exercises, you know where you're headed. I have a few final tips to help get you started.

■ *Looking for a Job?*

There are many excellent résumé books available in your university's library, so I won't even try to cover that topic here. Just remember, yet again, that everything is marketing. Your task is to sell your potential employer on the idea that you would be more valuable to his firm than anyone else he's considering. I'll show you a simple one hour task you can easily complete to distance yourself from the competition.

Research the firm for a full hour. Find every article published about the company's recent endeavors. Learn the company's history. Consult the numerous business directories in your library's reference section to learn about the structure of the company, its assets, market share, and primary products. Call the company's public relations department and ask for literature on the company's business mission and public financial statements. Be resourceful! Find out what aspects of the company's way of doing business are particularly well suited to your highly individual talents. Walk into your interview knowing more about the company than the recruiter does.

During the interview, don't worry too much about tooting your own horn. Your résumé, application, transcripts and letters of recommendation should take care of that for you. Let the interviewer know that you're well acquainted with the company and the industry. Show him why your talents are well suited to his firm so he has no doubt you'd be a fantastic employee. Now make him sell you on the idea of working for his company. Tell him you'd like to know why his company would be the best choice for you. After all, you'll be investing years of your life in the company and you want to make the right decision. Remember how you took your professors for a test drive? Do the same here. It's your future and you're in control.

■ *Going to Graduate School?*

I had fantastic success applying to graduate schools, due in large part to the guidance I received from Professor Fred Norman at the University of Texas at Austin. I give him credit for much of the information in this section. I applied to seven of the top fifteen graduate schools in economics, including the top three. Not only did they all admit me, each school offered me a full fellowship! $750,000 in fellowship offers, total. Wow! Too bad economics turned out to be such a disappointment!

Depending on your overall performance in college, you may or may not be able to expect such a great result. However, if you apply the techniques in this section you can make the most of your assets and get better admission offers than students with better transcripts from better schools.

There are four important parts to your application: transcripts, entrance exam scores, statement of purpose, and letters of recommendation. This entire book is targeted at improving your transcripts and cultivating good relationships with professors who will write your letters, so we won't discuss that here.

■ Entrance Exams

Practice, practice, practice! Nothing will improve your scores more than practicing taking the test under test conditions. The GRE is the most widely taken admissions exam. The single most essential aspect of the GRE verbal section is vocabulary. Memorize lots of vocabulary as I recommended earlier in the book and your verbal scores will soar. The math section verges on remedial. If your field uses a lot of math, this part of the test is a piece of cake for you already. If your field doesn't use math, then don't worry about it - the admissions people at your grad school won't care if you do poorly. The logic section is just a bunch of fun little games. Practice the games, learn to do them quickly and you're on easy street.

I've never taken the other tests like the LSAT, MCAT or GMAT. I'd recommend buying a good study guide for these tests as well as the GRE. Study and practice just as you would for any other important test. Study can and does improve your score, no matter what the test makers say.

■ *Statement of Purpose*

Here's where tactics come into play. Your statement of purpose describes what you regard to be your mission in graduate school. I have a great formula that worked well for me and everyone else I know who has used it.

First, research the schools to which you're considering applying. Find out what areas each school specializes in within your discipline. Ask each department's secretary to send you a list of the faculty and their areas of specialization. Look at their recent publications and select the topics that interest you the most. Keep a page of notes for each graduate school and write down everything you've discovered about the faculty's research interests that really appeals to you. You want to select the schools most appropriate for your talents and interests.

Next, create a three-pronged attack for each school. Your statement of purpose will be different for every program to which you apply. Why? Because when you get to the school, you'll want to make certain you make best use of the resources they have available, and every school is different. Your purpose will be slightly different at each school, so your statement should reflect it.

The first prong of the attack is a conventional field of endeavor - whichever shines most in the particular department. Express an interest in this recognized, conventional, safe specialization and state why you think that the particular graduate school to which you're applying is the best place to study it.

Next, pick an unusual but promising specialization that is prominent among the faculty. Show the admissions committee that you've researched their school and that you're sincerely interested in helping them further their studies in this field.

Finally, select a highly unconventional, cutting edge specialization of a member of the faculty. Ask your advisor to help you out here. You need to find something so new and promising that virtually no other under-graduates will have any clue about it. Demonstrate that through special study you have informed yourself and are extremely interested in learning more, and that you feel that their school is the best place for you to make your contribution.

You'll come across as extremely goal oriented, capable and well informed. The admissions committee will love you and throw money at you! Have fun!

¡Cebú! ?

EXERCISES

Bob the
tomato

1. Describe the life you want to be leading ten years from today. Where do you live? What sort of job are you working? Find something you like so much you'd do it for free.

I want to have a (big) house + be married and have a good paying job. I want to work with ~~elementary age~~ children (7 to 12). I want to help them grow-up + have fun.
I want to save the world + feed all the ~~starving~~ hungry people

Major : Psychology
※ ~~I want to be a child life specalist~~
∾ life coach
∾ counselor
? ∾ social worker
∾ Human Resources

∾ international humanitarian
∾ interpreter of foreign language(s)

learn languages : Korean, Spanish, Japanese, German

2. *on pg 9*

Why is college important, considering where you want to be in ten years? Will you be able to achieve what you want if you do poorly in college?

if I waste my time and do poorly in college I will not be satisfied with my life nor will I be able to get + keep the job I want. I'd be mad at myself.

College is important for me so I can get a career (or at least have a better chance).
I think education is the key to my future.

3. List at least five potential advisors who currently work in jobs you'd like to have. If you don't know anyone, list five people you know who could introduce you to someone. Contact all of these people during the next week. Nothing

① Susan Cordes Green → Psych prof. + advisor

② Merit Care - Fargo

③ Children's hospital (St. Paul ?)

④ Mrs. Jouppi (high school career lady)

⑤ Search the web → ask Jeeves ☺

1
2
3
4
5

4. Jump into the future where you achieve all of your goals and write your own college graduation announcement. What outrageous and powerful results did you produce?

During my four years at Concordia College I have not only accomplished my goals, but I have surpassed them. I never could have done it all without the help of wonderful, talented, and kindhearted friends. I have in circle (K) for the past 4 yrs and achieved the office of vice president; I have put together many successful service projects & recieved servant leader awards and a few scholarships. Throughout all my classes I have worked hard and achieved above average grades & a 3.7-3.8 gpA. I've made lasting relationships with several profs. and helped underclassmen. I have friends at every corner and a warm smile from every face. I've helped several lost sheep find their way back to God and his glorious love & light.

5. What if you don't work to achieve your goals? Instead you loaf, complain and whine. What will it feel like when you finally do manage to graduate? Write your announcement.

I can't believe I've finally made it. College was a joke + a big waste of time ... if only I'd paid attention in class maybe I could have learned something. What am I going to tell my employers? that I sleep for 6 yrs through All my classes?! And what did a gain? Nothing?
★If only I had read that book by Darin King "things would have been so much easier?

6. Create a blueprint for your education. Plan your classes all the way to graduation. Put a star next to every important prerequisite and be certain to take the class on time.

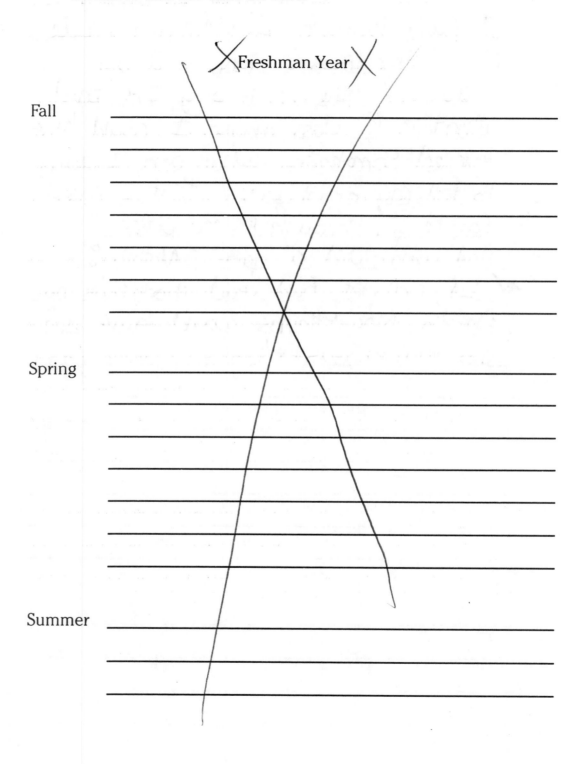

Freshman Year

Fall

Spring

Summer

Sophomore Year

Fall

Spring

Summer

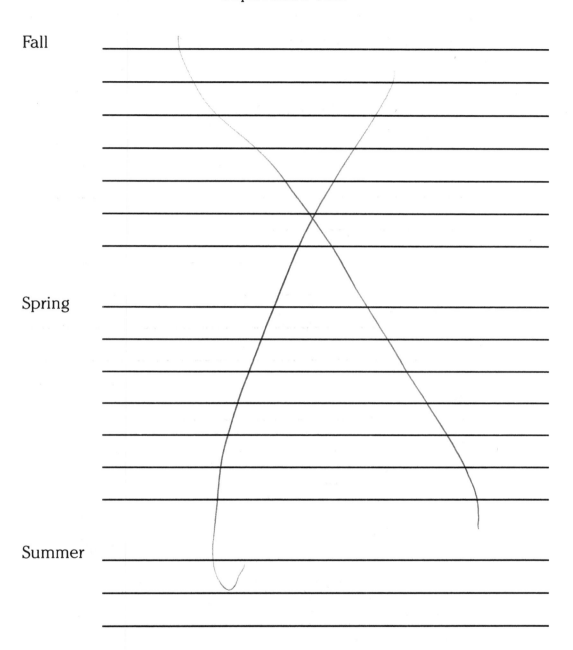

Senior
~~Junior~~ Year

Fall
2007

(1) Economics in Society
* Stats for Psych
* Abnormal Psych (461)
(R) Multi-Ethnic American Literature

12 credits

Spring
2008

* Psych 303 + 304
* Applied Behavior Analysis (Psych 402)
minor (R) Theatre History (COMM 285)

~ *Psych 318 Peace studies ~

12 credits

Summer

Senior Year

Fall
2008

_____
_____
_____
_____
_____
_____
_____

Spring
2009

_____
_____
_____
_____
_____
_____

* Need Directing I
* 404 senior capstone
* 494 Research

7. Think back to a time when you had an unusually effective study session. Recreate the experience vividly in your mind. Where were you sitting? How were you sitting? What kind of clothes were you wearing? Had you eaten recently? What time of day was it? How were you breathing? Describe as completely as possible the state of your body.

_____

_____

_____

_____

_____

_____

_____

_____

_____

_____

_____

_____

_____

_____

_____

_____

_____

8. While you're still in the same state, we'll perform the same exercise for your mind. What were you thinking? Were you talking to yourself? Was your mind clear? What did it feel like? What emotions were you experiencing?

---

9. Relive in your mind a test that you aced. Recreate the entire experience and make a mental movie out of it. Describe yourself - how were you using both your mind and your body?

_____

_____

_____

_____

_____

_____

_____

_____

_____

_____

_____

_____

_____

_____

_____

_____

_____

_____

Summary of Rules and Axioms

Chapter 1 Finding Your Direction

Rule #1 Find a future that excites you and motivates you to take action now!

Rule #2 Build a group of advisors from the field you want to pursue.

Rule #3 Seize complete control over your education immediately.

Rule #4 A goal is a specific, concrete, measurable objective that you find exciting.

Rule #5 Goals are nice, but they don't achieve themselves.

Rule #6 Use reverse visualization to discover what you must do to achieve your goals.

Rule #7 Large projects are much more easily achieved when broken up into manageable pieces.

Rule #8 Make action plans that allow you to take a step toward your goals every day.

Rule #9 Use your mind frequently to create a detailed vision of your goal attained.

Rule #10 Evaluate your actions periodically to make sure you're consistently working toward your goals.

Rule #11 Your persistence above all else will determine whether you achieve your goals.

Rule #12 You, and only you, are responsible for every result in your life.

Rule #13 Your future will be determined not by your past, but by the actions you are taking right now.

Rule #14 You must live with the consequences of every decision you make and every action you take.

Chapter 2 Reading Effectively

Rule #15 Know your mission before you begin reading.

Rule #16 PUCR-UP for effective reading!

Rule #17 Organize information before you try to learn it.

Rule #18 Get to know the book and author before you start reading.

Rule #19 Understand the author's goals, assumptions, methods and biases.

Rule #20 Discover the author's main points and highlight only the information that contributes directly to those main points.

Rule #21 Pause after each paragraph, section and chapter to recite in your own words the author's main ideas.

Rule #22 Recreate from memory an outline of the main ideas in the work.

Rule #23 Apply what you have learned to a problem immediately after you finish reading.

Rule #24 Fiction is all about the lives of characters. Understand the characters to discover what the author is trying to tell you about life.

Rule #25 Keep a vocabulary notebook to improve your reading and writing ability, grades, and conversational skills.

Chapter 3 Planning Your Semester

Rule #26 Think of your university as a business and yourself as a paying customer. Get what you pay for!

Rule #27 Know your degree requirements completely. Fight for the classes you need when you need them.

Rule #28 Good grades come easy in classes you love.

Rule #29 Take advantage of your university's credit by examination program and self- paced classes to graduate more quickly.

Rule #30 Professors are like used cars: the only way to know if they're any good is to test drive them.

Rule #31 If the class is important for your future, choose the professor who will provide you with the best education. If the class is an unimportant, uninteresting requirement, choose the easiest professor.

Rule #32 Register for one more class than you intend to take, then drop the class you like the least.

Rule #33 Take multiple classes from your favorite professors. Good grades and fantastic letters of recommendation will result.

Rule #34 Buy your books early and read the first few chapters in each before class begins.

Rule #35 Audit an extremely difficult class one semester in advance.

Rule #36 Make a master calendar so you can spot and plan for all potentially dangerous time conflicts.

Rule #37 Use your master calendar to create an action plan for each class.

Rule #38 Consult your action plans each week and take action to complete the most important tasks first.

Rule #39 Full exertion at the beginning of each semester pays off big.

Rule #40 Cut your losses short - drop that loser class.

Chapter 4 School Daze

Rule #41 Completing and understanding the background reading assignment before the lecture is essential to your success in school.

Rule #42 If you want an A, you have to sell the professor on the idea that you deserve it.

Rule #43 Be in class on time, and stay until the end of every single lecture.

Rule #43 Be in class on time, and stay until the end of every single lecture.

Rule #44 Minimize distractions by sitting in the front of the classroom.

Rule #45 Show your professor that you're alive by listening attentively and actively.

Rule #46 Spend 75% of your time in lecture listening to your professor to find his main points. Spend the other 25% writing those points down.

Rule #47 Make your presence in class felt, but never be a nuisance.

Rule #48 Ask questions that show the professor you're a serious, interested student.

Rule #49 Within one hour after the lecture, review, organize and fill in your notes.

Rule #50 Don't return to your dorm room or apartment between classes. Use the time to review your previous lecture or to prepare for your next one.

Rule #51 Always keep up in every class.

Chapter 5 A Formula for Fantastic Papers

Rule #52 Take as many writing classes as you can. They're good for you.

Rule #53 Find an unusual way to link your paper topic to something that interests you.

Rule #54 The ideal thesis is interesting, specific, researchable and debatable.

Rule #55 Go beyond the average sources if you expect more than an average grade. Make use of research librarians, footnotes, academic databases, the Internet, and interesting knowledgeable people.

Rule #56 Enlist the aid of your subconscious to write a better paper.

Rule #57 Create a free form outline to link all of your ideas.

Rule #58 Write at maximum speed - worry about grammar later.

Rule #59 Critique your paper harshly. Require organization, clarity, and concrete proof.

Rule #60 Learn English grammar and usage. There are no excuses for ignorance.

Rule #61 Use your paper's title to grab your professor's attention and arouse his curiosity.

Rule #62 Your professor's last impression before he assigns a grade is your conclusion. Save the best for last.

Rule #62 Your professor's last impression before he assigns a grade is your conclusion. Save the best for last.

Rule #63 An A paper always has a smooth professional appearance.

Rule #64 Every paragraph conveys a single thought.

Rule #65 Variety in structure makes your paper easier to read and more pleasing to the eye.

Rule #66 Simplicity and clarity make the grade

Rule #67 Concrete examples, illustrations and analogies strengthen your paper and make it more interesting to read.

Rule #68 Consult a book of quotations for thesis ideas.

Rule #69 When you're stuck, open a random book and relate what you
read to your problem.

Chapter 6 Dealing with Your Professor

Rule #70 Organize your thoughts and questions in writing before you see your professor.

Rule #71 Get your professor to take a personal interest in your education by asking his advice.

Rule #72 Learn the primary distinctions and findings of your professor's research.

Rule #73 Learn what problems academics in your subject are currently working on.

Rule #74 Time spent complaining is wasted. Use your time enthusiastically to complete all assignments you're given.

Rule #75 Give credit where credit's due: recognize the good professors.

Rule #76 Honesty isn't the best policy - it's the only policy.

Chapter 7 Improving Your Memory

Rule #77 Memory isn't a "thing." It's a learned skill.

Rule #78 If you want to master any skill, you must learn the principles, apply them when appropriate, and practice.

Rule #79 Discover which sense you use most during learning.

Rule #80 Restructure your learning experience to concentrate on your dominant learning sense.

Rule #81 When learning, use as many senses as possible to give yourself more ways to remember.

Rule #82 For effective study and maximum recall, space your study sessions over time.

Rule #83 Sleep after you study to remember more of what you learn.

Rule #84 You remember best what you organize in advance.

Rule #85 Associate new information with facts you already know to enhance understanding and recall.

Rule #86 Create an interesting image whenever you want to remember.

Rule #87 Jump start your memory by recreating or vividly imagining the context in which you learned.

Rule #88 Overlearn for fast and accurate recall under pressure.

Rule #89 Review important information at increasing intervals to impress it upon long term memory.

Rule #90 Use acrostics and acronyms to remember short lists of items.

Rule #91 Use the keyword mnemonic to quickly master foreign and native vocabulary.

Rule #92 Interaction, motion and exaggeration increase your imagery recall.

Rule #93 Use the link method to memorize a lecture or a long list of information.

Rule #94 Use the loci method to remember a speech or any long list of items.

Rule #95 Use the loci method to cure simple forgetfulness.

Rule #96 Use the peg system when you need to remember not only a
         list, but also the number of each item in the list.

Rule #97 Prepare for an open book test with the peg system.Rule #98
         Use the number to sound system to remember numbers or
         very large lists of information.

Rule #98 Use the number to sound system to remember numbers or
         very large lists of information.

Chapter 8 Studying for Maximum Results

Rule #99 Duplicate during study the external conditions you will find yourself in when you need to remember.

Rule #100 The effectiveness of your study session is determined by your state, which in turn is a result of the way you're using your mind and body.

Rule #101 You can put yourself into an effective state for study by changing the way you use your body.

Rule #102 Use your most productive hours for your most difficult tasks.

Rule #103 If you have difficulty staying awake, try some homework that requires you to write or type.

Rule #104 The results you get when you study are a direct result of the thoughts you project.

Rule #105 If you're interested, you can concentrate.

Rule #106 Sincerely pretend that you're interested for a few minutes, and you will have the ability to concentrate.

Rule #107 Absolute focus is the key to accomplishing a great deal in a short period of time.

Rule #108 Express in writing exactly what you hope to achieve every study session.

Rule #109 Alternate test and study sessions to obtain feedback on your progress.

Rule #110 Explain what you know to someone else and you truly understand.

Rule #111 Use leisure time activities as a reward for accomplishing your study goals.

Chapter 9 Preparing for Tests

Rule #112 Create a main idea outline for each class every week. Review the all of your outlines for the entire semester at the end of every week.

Rule #113 Constantly be on the lookout for potential test questions.

Rule #114 Obtain copies of your professor's tests from previous years.

Rule #115 Memorize several good quotes that you can apply to a variety of questions.

Rule #116 Concentrate on the details to prepare for an objective test.

Rule #117 Memorize the methodologies for solving every type of problem you'll encounter.

Rule #118 Prepare for an open book test just as you would for a closed book one.

Rule #119 Formulate answers to your semester's test question collection.

Rule #120 Practice your answers to the questions first in a no pressure environment, then under test conditions.

Rule #121 Use the different perspectives of other students to prepare yourself for the test.

Rule #122 Acknowledge worry as a signal to take immediate action to prepare yourself.

Rule #123 Mistakes are invitations to learn more. Once you take value from the mistake =and learn how to correct it, dismiss it from your memory.

Rule #124 Eat light before a test - preferably fruit.

Rule #125 Exercise before your test.

Rule #126 Prepare your materials in advance and get to the test on time.

Rule #127 Relax your body and anxiety disappears.

Rule #128 As Epictetus said, "Men are not afraid of things, but of how they view them."

Rule #129 A low grade only means that you need to change your actions in order to win the grade game.

Rule #130 A test is an opportunity either to stand still or to make progress.

Rule #131 When the feeling of inevitable success is strong enough, you can do no wrong.

Rule #132 Neatness and organization help you distance yourself from your competition on tests.

Rule #133 Preview the entire test and assign times to each part before you begin.

Rule #134 Give yourself instructions mentally as you take the test.

Rule #135 First finish all of the questions to which you're certain you know the answers.

Rule #136 Skip any problem that is giving you too much trouble.

Rule #137 Break any hard problem down into smaller pieces until you reach something you can solve.

Rule #138 If you were not able to finish, use the last ten minutes to submit outlines for problems you were unable to reach. Never leave anything blank.

Rule #139 Correct every test question you missed and record it in your notes.

Rule #140 Fight for your grade before your professor submits it to the registrar.

The Four Axioms of the Grade Game

Axiom #1 The Ballpark Rule: He who runs the Ballpark makes the Rules. Either play by his Rules, or change Ballparks.

Axiom #2 The Competition Rule: Your result will be determined by your standing relative to the other students in the class.

Axiom #3 Everything is marketing!

Axiom #4 Go the extra mile.

YOUR COMMENTS!

1. Did you enjoy this book?

2. What have you gained from applying these principles? Tell me your story!

3. What was the single most valuable thing you learned from this book?

4. What would you like to see added to this book?

5. What new topics would you like to see in another book?

I would greatly appreciate it if you would take a couple of minutes to answer these questions for me now. Add any other comments you may have as well. Email your response to:

kingd@hotmail.com or king@noblehouse.com.